STRENGTHENING YOUR GRIP
Essentials in an Aimless World

BIBLE STUDY GUIDE

From the Bible-teaching ministry of

Charles R. Swindoll

INSIGHT FOR LIVING

Charles R. Swindoll is a graduate of Dallas Theological Seminary and has served in pastorates in Texas, New England, and California, since 1963. He has served as senior pastor of the First Evangelical Free Church of Fullerton, California, since 1971. Chuck's radio program, "Insight for Living," began in 1979. In addition to his church and radio ministries, Chuck enjoys writing. He has authored numerous books and booklets on a variety of subjects.

Based on the outlines and transcripts of Chuck's sermons, the study guide text is coauthored by Ken Gire, a graduate of Texas Christian University and Dallas Theological Seminary. The Living Insights are written by Bill Butterworth, a graduate of Florida Bible College, Dallas Theological Seminary, and Florida Atlantic University.

Editor in Chief:
Cynthia Swindoll

Coauthor of Text:
Ken Gire

Author of Living Insights:
Bill Butterworth

Assistant Editors:
Glenda Schlahta and
Karene Wells

Copy Manager:
Jac La Tour

Copyediting Supervisor:
Marty Anderson

Copy Editor:
Kevin Moritz

Director, Communications Division:
Carla Beck

Project Manager:
Alene Cooper

Project Supervisor:
Cassandra Clark

Art Director:
Don Pierce

Production Artist:
Gary Lett

Designer:
Diana Vasquez

Typographer:
Bob Haskins

Print Production Manager:
Deedee Snyder

Unless otherwise identified, all Scripture references are from the New American Standard Bible, © The Lockman Foundation 1960, 1962, 1963, 1968, 1971, 1972, 1973, 1975, 1977. Used by permission.

An effort has been made to locate sources and obtain permission where necessary for the quotations used in this book. In the event of any unintentional omission, a modification will gladly be incorporated in future printings.

ISBN 0-8499-8407-6
Printed in the United States of America.
COVER PHOTOGRAPH: Paul Lewis

CONTENTS

INTRODUCTION

T he eighties have been described as the decade of aimlessness. Yesterday's slogans like "Remember Pearl Harbor!" and "We shall overcome!" have lost their capacity to martial our loyalty, clarify our goals, or strengthen our resolve. The shrill calls to join causes have been replaced with yawns of indifference and disrespect —even on the part of many Christians. We are seeing the sand castles that once housed our hopes washed out to sea.

But we don't have to be washed away with this tide. Instead, we can focus our aims anew on certain essentials, such as:

- Keeping priorities straight

- Staying involved with others

- Striving for purity of life

- Maintaining integrity

- Cherishing family life

Because these and other principles are based on eternal truths, they form fixed points that keep us from drifting aimlessly. God's eternal and essential principles must be firmly grasped and communicated afresh if we hope to survive.

If you are looking for a few essentials to grab hold of as your world seems to be spinning by, almost out of control, these studies are just for you.

Chuck Swindoll

PUTTING TRUTH INTO ACTION

Knowledge apart from application falls short of God's desire for His children. He wants us to apply what we learn so that we will change and grow. This study guide was prepared with these goals in mind. As you go through the following pages, we hope your desire to discover biblical truth will grow as your understanding of God's Word increases, and that you will be encouraged to apply what you've learned.

To assist you in your study, we've included a section called **Living Insights** at the end of each lesson. These exercises will challenge you to study further and to think of specific ways to put your discoveries into action.

There are many ways to use this guide—in personal devotions, group studies, discussions with friends and family, and Sunday school classes. And, of course, it's an ideal study aid when you're listening to its corresponding "Insight for Living" radio series.

To benefit most from this study guide, we would encourage you to consider it a spiritual journal. That's why we've included space in the **Living Insights** for recording your thoughts and discoveries. We hope you'll return to those sections often for review and encouragement as you continue to grow in your walk with Christ.

Ken Gire

Ken Gire
Coauthor of Text

Bill Butterworth
Author of Living Insights

STRENGTHENING YOUR GRIP
Essentials in an Aimless World

Chapter 1

STRENGTHENING YOUR GRIP ON PRIORITIES

1 Thessalonians 2:1–13

The church pulpit is much more than a polished podium from which a pastor can pontificate. Since the beginning of our Christian heritage, it has been the primary place where God's Word is dispensed to His people. From the pulpit His truth is proclaimed, His warnings are sounded, His people are fed.

But what governs the words of spiritual nourishment that come from the pulpit? *Priorities.* It's easy to see a church's priorities when the ministry is just starting out, when the ink of the congregation's ideals is still wet on the paper. But later on, when storms roll in, the priority list can get blown away in a gust of confusion.

To keep this list securely nailed down, we must strengthen our grip on four priorities—priorities that should characterize our churches as well as our personal lives.

Four Priorities That Characterize a Meaningful Ministry

As time passes, Christian organizations tend to lose their vitality. Like wineskins, they lose their pliancy, rigidly adhering to past procedures. As a result, they become provincial and ingrown. Writing to the church at Thessalonica, Paul gives four priorities that will help keep us spiritually vital.

The Ministry Must Be Biblical

The foundation of Paul's message was the gospel.

> For you yourselves know, brethren, that our coming to
> you was not in vain, but after we had already suffered
> and been mistreated in Philippi, as you know, we had

1

the boldness in our God to speak to you the gospel of God amid much opposition. For our exhortation does not come from error or impurity or by way of deceit; but just as we have been approved by God to be entrusted with the gospel, so we speak, not as pleasing men but God, who examines our hearts. (1 Thess. 2:1–4)

When Paul spoke to this church, it was with "the gospel of God"—not human rhetoric or opinion. The gospel was the foundation upon which the apostle built his exhortations and reproofs. Whenever a church concentrates on trying to please people instead of pleasing God, fissures form in its foundation. God's Word alone gives a church an authoritative blueprint. A church can be guided only by being faithful to His Word. The plumb line of practice must square with founding principles. This foundation must be biblically level in all areas: philosophy, educational curriculum, government, music, ministry, and messages. If a church's ministry isn't biblical, it will collapse the first time a trial shakes its foundation.

If you skip down to verse 13, you'll see how the Thessalonians responded to Paul's preaching.

And for this reason we also constantly thank God that when you received from us the word of God's message, you accepted it not as the word of men, but for what it really is, the word of God, which also performs its work in you who believe.

When the Word of God is proclaimed, God's people are fed— including the pastor. It falls like a seed on fertile soil. Once received, it takes root in our lives, grows, and produces fruit. Everyone benefits. Everyone is nurtured.

How receptive is the soil of your heart to His Word? Are there any rocks or weeds that are keeping it from taking root in your life? If so, won't you submit yourself to God's hoe and allow His Word to perform its work in your life (Heb. 4:12)?

The Ministry Must Be Authentic

Reflecting on the days he spent with the Thessalonian church, Paul recalls that he

never came with flattering speech, as you know, nor with a pretext for greed—God is witness—nor did we seek glory from men, either from you or from others, even though as apostles of Christ we might have asserted our authority. (1 Thess. 2:5–6)

Paul's ministry to the Thessalonians wasn't marred by egoism or exploitation. It was genuine and sincere. Likewise, our ministries must be free of deception and the desire to impress. Without hypocrisy. Without hype. We must be real—full of authenticity, not platitudes.

In the classic children's story *The Velveteen Rabbit,* the old Skin Horse explains to the Rabbit how to be real.

> "It doesn't happen all at once," said the Skin Horse. "You become. It takes a long time. That's why it doesn't often happen to people who break easily, or have sharp edges, or who have to be carefully kept. Generally, by the time you are Real, most of your hair has been loved off, and your eyes drop out and you get loose in the joints and very shabby. But these things don't matter at all, because once you are Real you can't be ugly, except to people who don't understand."[1]

How real are we with others? Are we willing to let our hair be loved off, willing to appear shabby? Are we willing to go through the pain of becoming real, even if it takes a long time? If we hide behind sewn-on smiles that mask our real feelings, so will the people around us. And our ministry will lose its meaning.

The Ministry Must Be Gracious

Paul wanted his message to be not only authentic but gracious as well—full of tenderness and compassion.

> But we proved to be gentle among you, *as a nursing mother tenderly cares for her own children.* Having thus a fond affection for you, we were well-pleased to impart to you not only the gospel of God but also our own lives, because you had become very dear to us. (vv. 7–8, emphasis added)

What is more tender than a mother nursing her child? Paul uses this image to convey a gentleness and compassion so often missing in present-day Evangelicalism. The pulpit shouldn't be a stainless-steel milk dispenser but a rocking chair, where the pastor lovingly nurses the church.

Paul knew that the Thessalonians needed more than the Word. He didn't shove a big, black King James down their throat; instead, he imparted the Word to them through his life as a mother imparts

---

1. Margery Williams, *The Velveteen Rabbit* (1983; reprint, New York, N.Y.: Alfred A. Knopf, 1986), p. 14.

milk to her nursing child through her own breasts. And like that mother, a pastor should teach with the utmost care, gentleness, and reverence.

Later, Paul shifts from a maternal metaphor to a paternal one.

> You are witnesses, and so is God, how devoutly and uprightly and blamelessly we behaved toward you believers; just as you know how we were exhorting and encouraging and imploring each one of you *as a father would his own children.* (vv. 10–11, emphasis added)

Just as we need a mother's love, so we need the love of a father who will take us by the hand and teach us how to walk. We need the strength of His hand not only to guide us but to pick us up when we stumble.

Just as a child needs a mother and a father, so we need grace and truth when presenting the Word of God to others.

The Ministry Must Be Relevant

Paul's message was relevant and applicable to every situation. Its truth wasn't theoretical but practical.

> So that you may walk in a manner worthy of the God who calls you into His own kingdom and glory. And for this reason we also constantly thank God that when you received from us the word of God's message, you accepted it not as the word of men, but for what it really is, the word of God, which also performs its work in you who believe. (vv. 12–13)

For a ministry to be meaningful, it must be relevant. It must answer today's issues today. It must look forward more often than back. It must be flexible, willing to break the constricting wineskins of tradition in order to stay fluid and in touch with current needs.

The Result of a Meaningful Ministry

Biblical accuracy . . . authenticity . . . graciousness . . . relevance. When these are priorities in ministry, our Christianity becomes incarnated in our lives rather than something we put on and take off, like a coat from the closet. It is something we assimilate, something that soaks into our lives so deeply and completely that it changes the very chemistry of our being. And only when we strengthen our grip on changing from the inside out will we significantly impact the world around us.

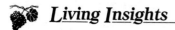 **_Living Insights_** STUDY ONE

Our study has revealed that a meaningful ministry is characterized by four priorities, which we found in 1 Thessalonians 2:1–13. Let's expand our biblical base. For each priority, do a little Scripture search, using a concordance. List other references, along with a key word or phrase, that support each priority.

The Ministry Must Be Biblical

References	Key Words
1 Thess. 2:1–4	

The Ministry Must Be Authentic

References	Key Words
1 Thess. 2:5–6	

The Ministry Must Be Gracious

References	Key Words
1 Thess. 2:7–11	

The Ministry Must Be Relevant

References	Key Words
1 Thess. 2:12–13	

Living Insights

We've discussed priorities that a church should consider important. Now let's ask the question, Am I living out these priorities?

- Review the four priorities—biblical accuracy, authenticity, graciousness, and relevance—and ask yourself the following questions.

    —Does my home possess and encourage those same qualities? Probe a bit, asking why or why not.

    —If these qualities are missing, what effect is their absence having in my home?

    —Can a person without these priorities change to embrace them? If so, what's the key?

    —What would people miss the most about me if I suddenly died? What one, single quality of mine would leave the greatest hole in their lives?

Chapter 2

STRENGTHENING YOUR GRIP ON INVOLVEMENT

Acts 2:42–47, Romans 12:9–16, 1 Corinthians 12:20–27

Seventeenth-century sage John Donne once wrote:

> No man is an island, entire of itself; every man is a piece of the continent, a part of the main; if a clod be washed away by the sea, Europe is the less . . . ; any man's death diminishes me, *because I am involved in mankind;* and therefore never send to know for whom the bell tolls; it tolls for thee.[1] (emphasis added)

Since we all are involved in mankind, how much more should we Christians be involved in the lives of other believers?

Verses like John 17:23 and 26 underscore the fact that love and unity should characterize our involvement with each other. These verses have inspired such lofty lyrics as "We are one in the Spirit, we are one in the Lord . . . they'll know we are Christians by our love."[2] But have these lyrics moved our lives as often as they've moved our lips?

A more down-to-earth chorus might be:

> To dwell above with saints we love,
> That will be grace and glory.
> To live below with saints we know;
> That's another story!
> (Author unknown)

In this lesson we want to get a better grip on our involvement with other Christians. Hopefully, by the end of our study, we'll all be singing another tune, one in harmony with each other.

---

1. John Donne, as quoted in *Bartlett's Familiar Quotations,* 15th ed., rev. and enl., ed. Emily Morison Beck (Boston, Mass.: Little, Brown and Co., 1980), p. 254.

2. Peter Scholtes, "They'll Know We Are Christians by Our Love" (Las Vegas, Nev.: F. E. L. Publications, 1966).

Involvement in God's Family—A Historical Glance

Throughout history, no church has better modeled involvement than the church in Acts 2. At the end of Peter's message on the Day of Pentecost, three thousand Jews were saved. They had no church building, no Bible, no seasoned pastor, no traditions or forms of church government. Yet this new congregation knew more about how a church should function than we do today with two thousand years of experience and libraries full of church history notes.

> And they were continually devoting themselves to the apostles' teaching and to *fellowship*, to the breaking of bread and to prayer. (Acts 2:42, emphasis added)

Initially drawn together by the thread of their common commitment to Christ, the early church members became a tightly knit group. The Greek term for *fellowship* is *koinōnia*, the root of which means "common."

Their Fellowship Analyzed

Verses 44–47 show us this *koinōnia* at work.

> And all those who had believed were together, and had all things *in common*; and they began selling their property and possessions, and were sharing them with all, as anyone might have need. And day by day continuing with one mind in the temple, and breaking bread from house to house, they were taking their meals together with gladness and sincerity of heart, praising God, and having favor with all the people. And the Lord was adding to their number day by day those who were being saved. (emphasis added)

First, fellowship was entered into by all. Not one of them had an island mentality (vv. 44–45). They shared everything they had: property, possessions, food, even their own lives (vv. 44, 46). Second, this sharing was sincere, not contrived or coerced. Their fellowship sparkled with authenticity (v. 46).

Their Fellowship at Work

The early church expressed its involvement—or *koinōnia*—in two ways. The people shared *with someone:* things like money, time, food, encouragement, reproof, confession. And they shared *in something:* a situation, an experience, a failure, an emotion. In all their times of need, they were never alone (Heb. 13:3).

As you look back at the involvement of the believers in Acts 2, how do you compare? Do you build bridges that link your life with others, or do you hermit yourself away on some isolated island? Even if you surround yourself with an archipelago of Sunday faces, you can still be lonely . . . for islands, however close in proximity, are still separated from each other. The only cure for loneliness is to build relational bridges to span the seas that separate you.

Involvement in God's Family—A Present Glance

In two other New Testament passages, Paul vividly describes the involvement in Acts 2 by answering the questions: Why should we be involved with others? Why should we open up our lives? Why take the risk?

God Commands It

In Romans 12:9–16, Paul delivers God's command to be involved.

> Let love be without hypocrisy. Abhor what is evil; cling to what is good. Be devoted to one another in brotherly love; give preference to one another in honor; not lagging behind in diligence, fervent in spirit, serving the Lord; rejoicing in hope, persevering in tribulation, devoted to prayer, contributing to the needs of the saints, practicing hospitality. Bless those who persecute you; bless and curse not. Rejoice with those who rejoice, and weep with those who weep. Be of the same mind toward one another; do not be haughty in mind, but associate with the lowly. Do not be wise in your own estimation.

God commands us to accept others as Christ accepted us (Rom. 15:7). How did He accept us? With open arms. He died on the cross not with His arms folded or behind His back, but with His arms out, ready to embrace us as we are. We, then, are to reach out to others with more than an arm's-length acceptance; we are to invite them with open arms into our homes and into our lives (Heb. 13:1–2).

The Body Needs It

God also commanded us to be involved with others because He knew we needed it. In 1 Corinthians 12 Paul develops the analogy:

> But now there are many members, but one body. And the eye cannot say to the hand, "I have no need of you"; or again the head to the feet, "I have no need of you." (vv. 20–21)

A hand is tough, yet an eye is tender. A body needs both tough and tender parts to be healthy and whole. It needs the eye to see a flicker of change on a face that the hand could never see. But it also needs the hand to be able to remove a speck from an ailing eye.

> There should be no division in the body, but that the members should have the same care for one another. And if one member suffers, all the members suffer with it; if one member is honored, all the members rejoice with it. Now you are Christ's body, and individually members of it. (vv. 25–27)

We need each other, for two specific reasons. First, *to dispel division* (v. 25a). Involvement breaks down cliques, mends fractures in fellowship, and halts the spread of destructive diseases (see also Eph. 4:15–16).

Second, *to cultivate compassion* (1 Cor. 12:25b–26). Involvement allows us to both suffer and rejoice with others. This kind of caring is a sign of good health (see also Rom. 12:15, Heb. 13:3).

Three Ingredients of Involvement

What does involvement include? From the passages we've studied today, three ingredients stand out.

Spontaneity

Involvement should be voluntary and spontaneous, never mandatory or contrived. When you learn of another's need, pick up that phone . . . write that letter . . . offer assistance. Build a bridge to that person's life.

Vulnerability

The word *vulnerable* means "capable of being . . . wounded, open to attack or damage."[3] Something beautiful happens when we open our wounded hearts to others and allow them to see our wounds. Then they can not only share our hurt, but also ease our pain (see also Gal. 6:1–2).

Accountability

When we're involved, we can no longer come and go without being responsible to others. We keep each other accountable to be godly, loving, and pure.

In *Where Is God When It Hurts*, Philip Yancey challenges us to be involved in the body.

---

3. *Webster's Ninth New Collegiate Dictionary*, see "vulnerable."

Loud screams of pain from the body of Christ. . . . are not always so far away: there are some in every church and office. The unemployed, divorced, widowed, bed-ridden, aged . . . are we listening to them?[4]

 ## Living Insights

Romans 12:9–16 and 1 Corinthians 12:20–27 leave no question about the importance of involvement. Let's do some further study.

- As you reread these verses, principles of involvement should quickly surface. Write them in the space provided.

Romans 12:9–16

Reference _____

Principle _____

_____

Reference _____

Principle _____

_____

Reference _____

Principle _____

_____

Reference _____

Principle _____

_____

Reference _____

Principle _____

_____

---

4. Philip Yancey, *Where Is God When It Hurts* (Grand Rapids, Mich.: Zondervan Publishing House, 1977), p. 170.

1 Corinthians 12:20–27

Reference _____

Principle _____

_____

Reference _____

Principle _____

_____

Reference _____

Principle _____

_____

Reference _____

Principle _____

_____

Reference _____

Principle _____

_____

 Living Insights _____ STUDY TWO

Where do you stand in the spectrum of involvement? If you're uninvolved, try to identify some barriers which keep you from relating to others. What steps could you take to get around these barriers?

- Take a moment to answer those questions. First, assess your level of involvement with others. If you see room for improvement, write down specific barriers to involvement that you can identify in your life. Then jot down some solutions for getting around the barriers.

Involvement and Me

How involved am I with others? (Rate yourself on a scale of 1 to 10, with 10 being highest.)

1   2   3   4   5   6   7   8   9   10

What are some barriers to that involvement?

_____

_____

_____

_____

_____

_____

What are some solutions to those barriers?

_____

_____

_____

_____

_____

_____

Chapter 3

STRENGTHENING YOUR GRIP ON ENCOURAGEMENT

Hebrews 10:19–25

Encourage me.

Maybe you haven't said it out loud in recent days. But chances are you have shaped the words in the silent hallways of your soul.

Encourage me. *Please.*

Maybe you haven't stopped anyone on the street and said that precise phrase. But if someone who cared enough looked close enough . . . they would see the words written in your frowning face, drooping shoulders, pleading eyes. They would hear the words echo in your unguarded comments and unsurpassed sighs.

If the truth were known, you're *craving* some encouragement. Looking for it. Longing for it. And probably grieving because you've found it in such short supply.

. . . Is that where you've been lately? Hibernating in the den of discouragement? Licking your wounds under some heavy, dark clouds that won't blow away? Thinking seriously about quitting the human race?

If so, you are undoubtedly running shy on reinforcement and affirmation these days. You are beginning to wonder not *when* relief is coming, but *if* it will ever come, right?[1]

B eing discouraged is one thing. Encouraging others at the same time is almost impossible. But, hopefully, if you are discouraged, today's lesson will extend a helping hand to pull you out of that pit of despair so you can strengthen your grip on encouraging others.

The Meaning of Encouragement

The word *encourage* is from a French word meaning "to put courage into." Webster defines the word as "to inspire with courage, spirit, or hope . . . to spur on."[2]

---

1. Charles R. Swindoll, *Encourage Me* (Portland, Oreg.: Multnomah Press, 1982), p. 7.
2. *Webster's New Collegiate Dictionary,* see "encourage."

14

Regardless of how important or influential a person may be, regardless of how secure or successful, encouragement is always needed and appreciated.

Always.

The Ministry of Encouragement

OK, take out a pencil and paper. Pop quiz: Why do believers gather together every Sunday?

Perhaps the first answers that come to your mind are "to worship God . . . to meet with Him . . . to hear His Word . . . to praise His name." If that's true, you're half right. The other half of the answer is found in Hebrews 10:19–25.

In verses 19–21, we are told what we *have:*

> We have confidence to enter the holy place by the blood of Jesus, by a new and living way which He inaugurated for us through the veil, that is, His flesh, and . . . we have a great priest over the house of God.

We have confidence in our approach to God because we have a high priest who gives us access to God. Before Calvary, the only way to come to God was with an animal sacrifice, and that approach was tainted with fear and trepidation. When Christ died, the veil of the temple was torn from top to bottom, and the believer had access into the holy of holies—the very throne of God.

Based on what we have, we are next instructed as to what we should *do:*

> Let us draw near with a sincere heart in full assurance of faith, having our hearts sprinkled clean from an evil conscience and our bodies washed with pure water. Let us hold fast the confession of our hope without wavering, for He who promised is faithful; and let us consider how to stimulate one another to love and good deeds, not forsaking our own assembling together, as is the habit of some, but encouraging one another; and all the more, as you see the day drawing near. (vv. 22–25)

First: *We should draw near to God's presence* (v. 22). We no longer need to tiptoe by the throne room of God or walk on eggshells in His presence. We are invited to walk boldly to God across the crimson carpet Jesus laid down for us.

Second: *We should hold fast to God's promises* (v. 23). The concept here is one of unswerving faith in the truth of God. If we can stand before the God of heaven without our knees knocking, certainly we can stand here on earth without buckling under to intimidating people or circumstances.

Remember, life was hard for the Hebrews too. Their faith came at great cost. Many were torn from their families. Many were imprisoned. Many were martyred. It would have been only natural for them to waver under the pressure of such circumstances. That's why they needed something firm and solid to cling to. And that stabilizer is the promises of God—the same thing that strengthened Abraham.

> With respect to the promise of God, he did not waver in unbelief, but grew strong in faith, giving glory to God, and being fully assured that what He had promised, He was able also to perform. (Rom. 4:20–21)

Third: *We should consider how to stimulate one another to produce love and good deeds* (Heb. 10:24). The word *consider* means "to fix one's mind or one's eye on something." In the same way, we're to concentrate our attention on how to encourage others to exhibit Christlike behavior.

The most intense need in the family of God never makes the church bulletin or the Sunday morning announcements. That need is encouragement—God's way of fanning the flame of a flickering faith.

But how can God use us to fan those dying fires?

Verse 25 gives us the answer.

> Not forsaking our own assembling together, as is the habit of some, but encouraging one another; and all the more, as you see the day drawing near.

So you see, there's more to assembling together than sitting in a pew, Sunday after Sunday, singing praises and saying prayers. Like the wooden beams of the cross, fellowship has both vertical and horizontal aspects. One reaches up to God. The other reaches out to people. Even on the cross, Jesus' head was raised to God, but His hands were outstretched to embrace humanity. Likewise, when we come together, we come to worship God *and* to encourage others.

The Significance of Encouragement

There's more to encouragement than a smile and a pat on the back. The word *encouraging* in Hebrews 10:25 comes from a combination of two words: *para*, meaning "alongside"; and *kaleō*, meaning "to call." Together they mean "to call alongside." From this compound we get the word *Paraclete*, which is another name for the Holy Spirit. In the Gospel of John, that term is used to describe His work as one called alongside as our Helper and Comforter.

> "But the Helper, the Holy Spirit, whom the Father will send in My name, He will teach you all things, and bring to your remembrance all that I said to you." (14:26)

> "But I tell you the truth, it is to your advantage that I go away; for if I do not go away, the Helper shall not come to you; but if I go, I will send Him to you." (16:7)

These verses shed radiant light on the role of an encourager. The picture is not of one who confronts us face-to-face but of one who comes alongside to walk with us, to put an arm around us, to listen sensitively, to lend a shoulder to cry on, and to give gracious words that uplift us.

When you encourage others, you come closer to the ministry of the Holy Spirit than by anything else you can do.

Questions Concerning Encouragement

Time to sharpen that pencil again for another quiz.

1. Is encouragement to be done only on Sundays during the weekly "assembling together," or more often than that?

Answer: Day after day, as Hebrews 3:12–13 indicates.

> Take care, brethren, lest there should be in any one of you an evil, unbelieving heart, in falling away from the living God. But encourage one another day after day, as long as it is still called "Today," lest any one of you be hardened by the deceitfulness of sin.

2. Should I wait and watch for a hint that encouragement is desired before acting, or should I take the initiative?

Answer: Take the initiative, as Romans 14:19 implies.

> So then let us pursue the things which make for peace and the building up of one another.

3. Do I need to do something big to encourage someone, or is it possible to encourage with a word or two?

Answer: Even a word, spoken sincerely, can lighten a load or lift the spirits, as Proverbs instructs us.

There is one who speaks rashly like the thrusts of a
    sword,
But the tongue of the wise brings healing. (12:18)

Anxiety in the heart of a man weighs it down,
But a good word makes it glad. (v. 25)

A man has joy in an apt answer,
And how delightful is a timely word! (15:23)

A good example of encouragement can be found in 1 Samuel
23:15–16. The man in need of such a word is the renowned David,
a man you would think would be the last to need encouragement.
But such was not the case. When we pick up the story in verse 15,
he is running for his life, hunted and haunted by King Saul, who is
insane with jealousy and intent on killing David.

Now David became aware that Saul had come out to
seek his life while David was in the wilderness of Ziph
at Horesh. (v. 15)

When David heard about Saul's plans, doubtless he was shattered.
But a friend picked up those fragments and tenderly pieced them
back together.

And Jonathan, Saul's son, arose and went to David at
Horesh, and encouraged him in God. (v. 16)

Even David needed encouragement. Even a man after God's own
heart. And so does each of us.

Some Practical Suggestions for Encouraging Others

What are some specific ways to encourage? By observing and
mentioning admirable qualities you see in a person. Some of those
qualities might be an attention to details, faithfulness, a sweet smile,
a positive spirit, hard work, a good attitude, tactfulness, thoughtful-
ness, loyalty, thoroughness, or generosity. When you see good qualities, use them as a reason to express your appreciation for that person.

And finally, as Paul tells us in Ephesians 4:29, realize the awe-
some responsibility we have for one another—that God dispenses
his grace to others through our words of encouragement.

Let no unwholesome word proceed from your mouth,
but only such a word as is good for edification according to the need of the moment, that it may give grace
to those who hear.

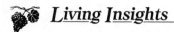

We defined encouragement as putting courage into someone, in-spiring a person with courage, spirit, or hope. Can you think of any-one in the Scriptures who could genuinely be called an "encourager"?

- As you look through your Bible, jot down the names of men and women who were encouragers and list how they encouraged others. Use a concordance if you need help.

Encouragers

_____

_____

_____

_____

_____

_____

_____

_____

_____

_____

_____

_____

_____

_____

_____

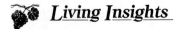

Now that we've seen some encouragers from the past, let's look for them in our lives today. Can you think of people you know who fit into this category?

- Take this time to name some people you know who encourage others, and list how they encouraged you. Then thank those people with a letter or phone call. This way, you will encourage someone with the encouragement you have received (2 Cor. 1:3–4).

Encouragers

_____

_____

_____

_____

_____

_____

_____

_____

_____

_____

_____

_____

_____

_____

_____

_____

_____

_____

_____

_____

Chapter 4

STRENGTHENING YOUR GRIP ON PURITY

1 Thessalonians 4:1–12

William Barclay writes in his commentary on 1 Thessalonians:

> One thing Christianity did was to lay down a completely new code in regard to the relationship of men and women; it is the champion of purity.[1]

Champion. The word means "one that does battle for another's rights or honor."[2] It conjures up images of King Arthur's Round Table—noble knights clad in shining armor, white horses draped with regalia, lances glinting in the sun as the knights charge off to use their might for right and to rescue damsels in distress.

For the Christian, the damsel in distress is purity, and Christianity is the knight in shining armor. But lately, it seems, the armor has grown rusty, and the knight has grown a little flabby around the middle—a case of too much sitting on the horse and not enough swinging of the sword.

For the individual believer, living a pure life is a matter of the will, as Paul tells us in Romans 6:12–13.

> Therefore do not let sin reign in your mortal body that you should obey its lusts, and do not go on presenting the members of your body to sin as instruments of unrighteousness; but present yourselves to God as those alive from the dead, and your members as instruments of righteousness to God.

Strong, bold commands to pick up the sword and confront the dragons of our desires. Fortunately, when our hands grasp the hilt of the sword, the hands of Christ wrap around ours to give us the strength to wield it more powerfully than we ever could on our own.

---

1. William Barclay, *The Letters to the Philippians, Colossians, and Thessalonians*, rev. ed., The Daily Study Bible Series (Philadelphia, Pa.: Westminster Press, 1975), p. 199.

2. *Webster's New Collegiate Dictionary*, see "champion."

And how we need that power within us, because the gauntlet thrown down against purity has never been more direct or challenging.

Moral Erosion: An Inescapable Fact

As we turn back the pages of history to the first century, we find a scene that is shockingly similar to the present day.

> In Rome for the first five hundred and twenty years of the Republic there had not been a single divorce; but now under the Empire, as it has been put, divorce was a matter of caprice. As Seneca said, "Women were married to be divorced and divorced to be married." In Rome the years were identified by the names of the consuls; but it was said that fashionable ladies identified the years by the names of their husbands. Juvenal quotes an instance of a woman who had eight husbands in five years. Morality was dead.
>
> In Greece immorality had always been quite blatant. Long ago Demosthenes had written: "We keep prostitutes for pleasure; we keep mistresses for the day-to-day needs of the body; we keep wives for the begetting of children and for the faithful guardianship of our homes." So long as a man supported his wife and family there was no shame whatsoever in extra-marital relationships.[3]

"No shame whatsoever." That's the epitaph that both of these cultures share with ours. For Greece and Rome, that epitaph is chiseled in granite. But for us, there is still time to affect our culture for Christ. And we can begin, as the popular song goes, "with the man in the mirror," for a better world, quite literally, begins with a better me.

Moral Purity: An Attainable Goal

Paul's message to the Thessalonian church was a call to champion the cause of purity, to pick up the sword and make a sharp break with the decadence of their culture.

> Finally then, brethren, we request and exhort you in the Lord Jesus, that, as you received from us instruction as to how you ought to walk and please God (just as you actually do walk), that you may excel still more. For you know what commandments we gave you by

3. Barclay, *The Letters to the Philippians, Colossians, and Thessalonians*, p. 199.

the authority of the Lord Jesus. For this is the will of God, your sanctification; that is, that you abstain from sexual immorality.[4] (1 Thess. 4:1–3)

All of us struggle from time to time trying to understand God's will for our life. But tucked away almost like a letter in a bureau drawer is the most explicit statement in Scripture on the will of God: "Abstain from sexual immorality."

The word *immorality* comes from the Greek word *porneia*. We get the term *pornography* from it. It means "fornication" and includes all forms of sexual sins.

Verses 4–5 show the two ways we can use our bodies—as vessels of honor or dishonor.

> That each of you know how to possess his own vessel
> in sanctification and honor, not in lustful passion, like
> the Gentiles who do not know God.

The essential point to understand about purity is that it requires us to exert control over our bodies. We must become our body's master, not its slave.

As Christians, we have a tendency to focus on the spiritual rather than the physical side of our being. Scripture, however, is quite forthright in talking about our bodies.

We are to present our bodies as living sacrifices to God (Rom. 12:1). We are not to yield our bodies to sin (6:12–13); in fact, we are told to flee immorality because our bodies are members of Christ and temples of the Holy Spirit (1 Cor. 6:15, 18–19). Consequently, our responsibility is to use our bodies for the glory of God (v. 20).

In light of these high commands, 1 Thessalonians 4:4 becomes extremely important. We are to be students of how physical stimuli affect our bodies. We need to know where we're vulnerable and where the danger zones are. Rest assured, if we don't know where our Achilles' heel is, Satan does. And that's just where he'll aim his arrow of temptation.

Whether your life turns out to be like verse 4 or like verse 5 depends on your ability to discriminate between good and evil. In reference to that, Paul gives us some wise counsel in 5:21–22.

> But examine everything carefully; hold fast to that
> which is good; abstain from every form of evil.

4. *Sanctification* means "the state of being set apart to God." A synonym would be the word *distinction*.

Just as we make discriminating choices in the grocery store between a good tomato and a rotten one, so we need to make wise choices about what we feed ourselves spiritually.

In Paul's letter to Titus, the apostle walks us down the aisle to help us know what to put in our shopping cart and what to leave on the shelf.

> For the grace of God has appeared, bringing salvation to all men, instructing us to deny ungodliness and worldly desires and to live sensibly, righteously and godly in the present age, looking for the blessed hope and the appearing of the glory of our great God and Savior, Christ Jesus; who gave Himself for us, that He might redeem us from every lawless deed and purify for Himself a people for His own possession, zealous for good deeds. (2:11–14)

There's that word again—that He might "*purify* for Himself a people for His own possession." Distinctly His. Uniquely His. Isn't that wonderful? Isn't that worth walking straight on by the passing pleasures of sin?

Peter echoes a similar thought.

> Therefore, gird your minds for action, keep sober in spirit, fix your hope completely on the grace to be brought to you at the revelation of Jesus Christ. As obedient children, do not be conformed to the former lusts which were yours in your ignorance, but like the Holy One who called you, be holy yourselves also in all your behavior; because it is written, "You shall be holy, for I am holy." (1 Pet. 1:13–16)

Moral Correction: A Biblical Mandate

Since God wants a pure people and since the church is a living representation of the body of Jesus Christ, then what's to be done with those members of the body that willfully choose to live impure lives?

In Matthew 18 Jesus outlines the steps we should take to reach out to such a person.

> "And if your brother sins, go and reprove him in private; if he listens to you, you have won your brother. But if he does not listen to you, take one or two more with you, so that by the mouth of two or three witnesses

every fact may be confirmed. And if he refuses to listen to them, tell it to the church; and if he refuses to listen even to the church, let him be to you as a Gentile and a tax-gatherer." (Matt. 18:15–17)

The advice reads like a step-by-step approach from a Christian counseling textbook. *Step one:* You go alone, in private, and confront the person. If there is no change, you go on to the next stage. *Step two:* You go again, this time with one or two witnesses. If there is still no change, you proceed to the next step. *Step three:* You make the matter public to the church. If there is still no change, you treat the person as an unregenerate.

Sounds harsh, doesn't it? Yet listen to the words of Dietrich Bonhoeffer, a man who was the epitome of Christian compassion.

> Ultimately, we have no charge but to serve our brother, never to set ourselves above him, and we serve him even when we must speak the judging and dividing Word of God to him, even when, in obedience to God, we must break off fellowship with him. We must know that it is not our human love which makes us loyal to the other person, but God's love which breaks its way through to him only through judgment. Just because God's Word judges, it serves the person.[5]

It's important to note that this extreme form of discipline is done only after all other means have been exhausted. And it's never done to devastate the person. It's done to bring restoration of the fallen Christian, to preserve the purity of the local church, and to be obedient to the Word of God.

In 1 Corinthians 5 we see this principle applied to a specific situation regarding the moral impurity of one of the church's members.

> It is actually reported that there is immorality among you, and immorality of such a kind as does not exist even among the Gentiles, that someone has his father's wife. And you have become arrogant, and have not mourned instead, in order that the one who had done this deed might be removed from your midst. For I, on my part, though absent in body but present in spirit, have already judged him who has so committed this, as though I were present. In the name of our Lord

5. Dietrich Bonhoeffer, *Life Together* (New York, N.Y.: Harper and Row, Publishers, 1954), p. 107.

Jesus, when you are assembled, and I with you in spirit, with the power of our Lord Jesus, I have decided to deliver such a one to Satan for the destruction of his flesh, that his spirit may be saved in the day of the Lord Jesus. Your boasting is not good. Do you not know that a little leaven leavens the whole lump of dough? Clean out the old leaven, that you may be a new lump, just as you are in fact unleavened. (vv. 1–7a)

Moral Inventory: A Look Inward

Purity involves more than a passing glance to see how much dirt we have under our fingernails. It requires a good, soaped-up, scrubbed-down Saturday night bath.

Where can we go to get that kind of cleansing? To Jesus.

If we say that we have fellowship with Him and yet walk in the darkness, we lie and do not practice the truth; but if we walk in the light as He Himself is in the light, we have fellowship with one another, and the blood of Jesus His Son cleanses us from all sin. If we say that we have no sin, we are deceiving ourselves, and the truth is not in us. If we confess our sins, He is faithful and righteous to forgive us our sins and to cleanse us from all unrighteousness. (1 John 1:6–9)

When we are willing to walk in the light and expose all the dirt in our lives, Jesus is there with the soap and washcloth "to cleanse us from *all* unrighteousness." He doesn't make us 99⁴⁴/₁₀₀ percent Ivory pure, but 100 percent pure.

A lot of religions teach morals. Only Christ offers forgiveness and total cleansing when those morals have been transgressed.

 Living Insights

Helping someone deal with impurity is a delicate matter. Let's consult some additional Scripture references to increase our understanding.

- Turn to Galatians 6:1–2 and jot down how these verses help you in confronting others and in being confronted yourself.

_____

_____

_____

_____

_____

- Now look at 1 Corinthians 5:9–13. When should this counsel be applied?

_____

_____

_____

_____

🍇 *Living Insights*

Let's take a few minutes to look at both sides of the coin: the positive side of purity and godliness, and the negative side of sinning and backsliding.

- How does godliness relate to purity? How do they differ? Are godliness and purity confined to any particular activities?

_____

_____

_____

_____

- What happens to a life when it becomes scarred by a lengthy period of backsliding? Can godliness be restored to the same level once a believer backslides?

_____

_____

_____

_____

Chapter 5

STRENGTHENING YOUR GRIP ON MONEY

1 Timothy 6:3–19

"Yeah, right. I wouldn't mind strengthening my grip on a briefcase of money," you say. But lest the title make a promise it can't deliver on, the lesson today is not about money grabbing! It offers no get-rich-quick formulas. It won't help you get your hands on a low-interest mortgage. And it won't help you understand APRs or ATMs, IRAs or the IRS.

What it will help you with, however, is getting a firm grasp on what the Bible says about money. And it says a lot. Surprisingly, giving is only one of the subjects it addresses. It talks about the nature of money as well as the nature of man in relation to money. It talks of spending, saving, and investing.

No matter how greatly monetary systems have changed since the Bible was penned, God's principles regarding money are still applicable. Today, we want to try on some of those ancient principles to see just how well they fit in today's ever-changing world of yen and francs, of dollar signs and decimal points.

The passage that will serve as our text is found in 1 Timothy 6. In it, we'll find a reminder to those who are *not* rich (vv. 6–8), a warning to those who want to *get* rich (vv. 9–10), and some instructions to those who *are* rich (vv. 17–19).

A Reminder to Those Who Are Not Rich

From a biblical point of view, money is amoral—neither moral nor immoral. It's the human heart and our attitude toward money that determines the issue of morality or immorality. Godliness is validated neither by wealth nor poverty. The Bible is replete with godly people who were poor—for example, John the Baptist (Matt. 3:4) and the widow who gave her last penny to the temple treasury (Mark 12:42). The Bible is also full of godly people who were rich— Abraham (Gen. 24:34–35) and Job (Job 1:1–3), for instance.

Paul addresses the subject of riches in 1 Timothy 6. Drawing from the word *godliness* in verses 3 and 5, Paul is quick to show in

28

verse 6 that gaining godliness is a higher goal than gaining anything of material merit.

But godliness actually is a means of great gain, when accompanied by contentment.

Godliness + Contentment = Great Gain

This formula for success would never make the cover story of *Forbes* or *Money* magazines. The great wealth spoken of here is a wealth that rust can't destroy or thieves steal (Matt. 6:19–20). A consistent and authentic walk with God *plus* an attitude of satisfaction and inner peace . . . that's what constitutes great wealth.

What, then, is necessary to help us quit striving for more and be contented and at peace with what we have?

The first half of the answer is found in 1 Timothy 6:7.

For we have brought nothing into the world, so we cannot take anything out of it either.

Babies are born empty-handed, and who ever saw a hearse pulling a U-Haul? That's why Paul tells us in Colossians 3:2 to "set your mind on the things above, not on the things that are on earth." We are to have an eternal perspective.

Having our sights telescoped on things above will cause our material longings to blur into the periphery. That's when we can relax—when our real needs are brought into focus.

And if we have food and covering, with these we shall be content. (1 Tim. 6:8)

So, to those who are not rich, the advice is clear. First, we need an eternal perspective (v. 7), and second, we need a simple acceptance of the essentials (v. 8).

And what are these essentials? Food and coverings.[1] With these we should be content, as Paul says in Philippians 4:11–13.

Not that I speak from want; for I have learned to be content in whatever circumstances I am. I know how to get along with humble means, and I also know how to live in prosperity; in any and every circumstance I have learned the secret of being filled and going

---

1. The word *covering* in verse 8 is a general word meaning "a covering overhead as well as a covering over our body." Therefore, living quarters as well as clothes are in view here (see also Matt. 6:24–34).

hungry, both of having abundance and suffering need.
I can do all things through Him who strengthens me.

Contentment, as verse 11 indicates, is something to be learned; and, as verse 13 says, it is something that can be done with the strength of Christ.[2]

Warning to Those Who Want to Get Rich

In verses 9–10 of 1 Timothy 6, the pronoun shifts from "we" to "those." Paul is addressing those who have made it their ambition to follow the rainbow's end in a frenzied search for that elusive, often illusory, pot of gold.

But those who want to get rich fall into temptation
and a snare and many foolish and harmful desires which
plunge men into ruin and destruction. (v. 9)

The term *want* seems tame enough in verse 9, but in the original Greek it indicates "resolve" or "determination." So for this person, the pursuit of money is not a passing fancy but a passionate obsession. For those possessed individuals, this verse offers a series of stern warnings:

First: They fall into temptation and a snare.

Second: They fall into many foolish and harmful desires.

Third: Those things plunge them into ruin and destruction.

The only other place in the New Testament where the Greek word for "plunge" is used is in Luke 5:7. There it refers to a boat about to sink. That gives a clear picture of how a person's life can go under in the course of a full-sailed pursuit of riches (compare Prov. 28:22).

Verse 10 of 1 Timothy 6 tells us that it is not money itself that is the problem, but the intimacy of our relationship with it.

For the love of money[3] is a root of all sorts of evil, and
some by longing for it have wandered away from the
faith, and pierced themselves with many a pang.

Notice this verse carefully—it does not say money is the root of *all* evil. Nor that the love of money is *the* root of evil. Love of money is *a* root, not *the* root, of *all sorts* of evil.

---

2. Contextually, the "all things" of Philippians 4:13 probably refers back to verse 12, which includes being able to live in the broad spectrum of circumstances ranging from poverty to prosperity.

3. Literally, "fondness of silver."

The term *longing* in verse 10 means "stretching oneself out in order to reach or grasp something." Two perils befall those who long for money: spiritually, they wander away; personally, they open a Pandora's box of problems. The picture here is of driven people wandering off the path into a veritable briar patch of thorns and nettles that repeatedly pierce them, causing severe pain.

In verse 11, Paul issues a warning for the godly: "Flee from these things." And in verses 11–16 he points us in the direction our lives should take—the righteous path that leads ultimately to Jesus.

Whether you're an up-and-coming young executive, or a parent with growing expectations for your family, or an older person scrambling to build a larger retirement fund, you can be flirting with the world and on the brink of a love affair with money. If so, these verses are ones to take to heart. Remember, in the end materialism will either cripple you or kill you.

Instructions for Those Who Are Rich

Paul now turns his attention away from the frustrated have-nots to the financially endowed. In doing so, he offers three pieces of advice in verses 17–19: two negative and one positive.

> Instruct those who are rich in this present world not
> to be conceited or to fix their hope on the uncertainty
> of riches, but on God, who richly supplies us with all
> things to enjoy. (v. 17)

First: *Don't be conceited.* Conceit is the first temptation money throws across our path, to become highbrowed and look down our nose at others who are not so well-heeled.

Second: *Don't trust in your wealth for security.* As Proverbs 23:4–5 warns,

> Do not weary yourself to gain wealth,
> Cease from your consideration of it.
> When you set your eyes on it, it is gone.
> For wealth certainly makes itself wings,
> Like an eagle that flies toward the heavens.

Third: *Become a generous person.*

> Instruct them to do good, to be rich in good works,
> to be generous and ready to share, storing up for them-
> selves the treasure of a good foundation for the future,
> so that they may take hold of that which is life indeed.
> (1 Tim. 6:18–19)

31

Such generosity not only allows a person to store up spiritual riches in heaven, it also gives that person the capacity to understand the true meaning of life.

Christ voices similar words in Luke 12:15.

> Beware, and be on your guard against every form of greed; for not even when one has an abundance does his life consist of his possessions.

What the whole world really longs for is not an abundance of things but an abundant life. So often, however, that longing drives us to all the wrong places, off the right road to wander somewhere in the tall weeds and tangled overgrowth.

ABUNDANT LIFE. The sign points only one way—to Jesus, who said,

> I came that they might have life, and might have it abundantly. (John 10:10b)

 ## Living Insights

The Bible certainly doesn't ignore the subject of money. In fact, many passages establish a basis for an appropriate mindset toward money. Let's look at some of them.

- Using your Bible and a concordance, look under the references *money*, *riches*, *wealth*, and *treasure*. For each reference, jot down several passages and state the principles you draw from them.

Money in the Bible

Reference: *money*

Passage: _____ Principle: _____

_____

_____

Passage: _____ Principle: _____

_____

_____

Passage: _____ Principle: _____

_____

_____

Passage: _____ Principle: _____

_____

_____

Reference: *Riches*

Passage: _____ Principle: _____

_____

_____

Passage: _____ Principle: _____

_____

_____

Passage: _____ Principle: _____

_____

_____

Passage: _____ Principle: _____

_____

_____

Reference: *Wealth*

Passage: _____ Principle: _____

_____

_____

Passage: _____ Principle: _____

_____

_____

Passage: _____ Principle: _____

_____

_____

Passage: _____ Principle: _____

_____

_____

Reference: *Treasure*

Passage: _____ Principle: _____

_____

_____

Passage: _____ Principle: _____

_____

_____

Passage: _____ Principle: _____

_____

_____

Passage: _____ Principle: _____

_____

_____

 Living Insights STUDY TWO

Sometimes it's not *adversity* that causes the Christian to struggle, but *prosperity*. Is this the case in your life? Discuss the following with your family or friends.

- Heavy artillery from our world pounds away on our eyes and ears. The media barrages us with a constant message. What is it? The next few times you watch television, pay close attention to the commercials. Behind the creative camera shots and clever dialogue is a powerful pitch. As it unfolds, talk about what message it's sending to you, the viewer.

- Are you caught up in the syndrome of living beyond your means? What steps are you taking to change those habits? Are you any further along toward financial stability than you were, say, one year ago? Two years ago? Define your greatest weakness in handling money.

- Pray specifically that the Lord Jesus Christ might be the Master of your money . . . how you earn it, where you spend it, when and to what you give it, why you save and invest it. Make Christ the Lord of your treasure.

Chapter 6

STRENGTHENING YOUR GRIP ON INTEGRITY

Psalms 75:5–7, 78:70–72

D r. Evan O'Neill Kane was chief surgeon of New York City's Kane Summit Hospital when he made a breakthrough that altered the thinking of the medical profession.

During his vast experience in surgery, Dr. Kane had seen a number of deaths and disabilities resulting from general anesthesia. It was his studied opinion that most major operations could be done under local anesthesia, a safer, more reliable method.

After performing nearly four thousand appendectomies with general anesthesia, Dr. Kane decided to conduct an experiment by removing an appendix with only local anesthesia.

Understandably, there wasn't a long line of volunteers. But that didn't stop the determined surgeon. On February 15, 1921, Dr. Kane performed this operation . . . on himself. The experiment was an overwhelming success. He recovered so rapidly that he was released from the hospital after just two days.

In today's chapter, we want *you* to operate on yourself. It will be painful, but unless we're each willing to undergo this type of surgery, the epidemic absence of integrity that's sweeping our world will never be stopped.

Two Tests

In the process of exploratory surgery, we want to administer a couple of tests—the test of adversity and the test of prosperity.

The Test of Adversity

There is nothing like adversity to reveal how strong or weak we are.

> If you are slack in the day of distress,
> Your strength is limited. (Prov. 24:10)

Whether you finish first in a marathon or have to rest after taking out the garbage is determined by your strength and stamina. And that is directly related to how well your heart is ticking.

How healthy is yours? How strong is it when the inclines of life start getting steeper? Adversity is like that uphill slope. The steeper the incline, the harder it is to keep running.

In *A Long Obedience in the Same Direction,* there is a profound statement about the role of adversity in our lives.

> [The] simplest and most ancient of human truths: namely, that life is an arduous and tragic struggle; that what we call 'sanity' . . . has a great deal to do with competence, earned by struggling for excellence; with compassion, hard won by confronting conflict; and with modesty and patience, acquired through silence and suffering.[1]

Job is a perfect illustration. Reading through the tearstained journal of Job's suffering, we find ten fresh graves on a windswept hill not far from his home. They are the graves of his children. One by one, Satan has taken them away, along with everything else he had—his livestock, his servants (Job 1:13–17), and now, finally, his health (2:7–8).

Several of Job's friends come to comfort him and give counsel. At first, they tiptoe gingerly around the ash heap in which he mournfully sits. But as time wears on, they start kicking up some dust of their own.

> Then Eliphaz the Temanite answered,
> "If one ventures a word with you, will you become
>   impatient?
> But who can refrain from speaking?
> Behold you have admonished many,
> And you have strengthened weak hands.
> Your words have helped the tottering to stand,
> And you have strengthened feeble knees.
> But now it has come to you, and you are impatient;
> It touches you, and you are dismayed." (4:1–5)

Patience wears thin under the abrasive rub of adversity, even for the most righteous of people. And if that rub is hard enough, coarse enough, or goes on long enough, dismay starts showing through the frayed fabric of our life.

---

1. Thomas Szasz, as quoted by Eugene H. Peterson, *A Long Obedience in the Same Direction* (Downer's Grove, Ill.: InterVarsity Press, 1980), pp. 16–17.

The Test of Prosperity

Believe it or not, adversity is a grade-school test compared to prosperity. Prosperity is graduate-level work. Scottish essayist Thomas Carlyle once said: "Adversity is sometimes hard upon a man; but for one man who can stand prosperity, there are a hundred that will stand adversity."[2] For you see, adversity tests one's ability to survive; prosperity tests one's integrity. Adversity simplifies life by reducing it to the basics; prosperity complicates it.

As the scalpel begins to cut into your life, I want you to look for integrity. Do you find it? Or do you see pride instead, spreading its cancerous rhizomes throughout your life?

If you had to answer "pride," God has a frank word of warning for you.

"Do not lift up your horn on high,
Do not speak with insolent pride." (Ps. 75:5)

If you're prospering, God warns: *Don't be conceited.* Don't toot your own horn. Since Solomon was something of a resident expert on prosperity, you might be tempted to go to him for a second opinion. But his advice is the same as in this psalm.

Let another praise you, and not your own mouth;
A stranger, and not your own lips. . . .
The crucible is for silver and the furnace for gold,
And a man is tested by the praise accorded him.
(Prov. 27:2, 21)

The second warning given in Psalm 75 is: *Keep the right perspective.*

For not from the east, nor from the west,
Nor from the desert comes exaltation;
But God is the Judge;
He puts down one, and exalts another. (vv. 6–7)

Whether you're in the valley or on the mountaintop, the tilt of the neck should be the same—you have to look up to see God. He is the judge over all the earth. He is the one, ultimately, who gives or takes away, who raises up or brings down (1 Sam. 2:7, Dan. 2:21).

A beautiful example of this is found in Psalm 78, where God took David as a humble young shepherd and exalted him to the highest office in the land.

---

2. *Bartlett's Familiar Quotations*, 15th ed., rev. and enl., ed. Emily Morison Beck (Boston, Mass.: Little, Brown and Co., 1980), p. 474.

He also chose David His servant,
And took him from the sheepfolds;
From the care of the ewes with suckling lambs He
    brought him,
To shepherd Jacob His people,
And Israel His inheritance.
So he shepherded them according to the integrity of
    his heart,
And guided them with his skillful hands. (vv. 70–72)

David wasn't a mover and shaker. He wasn't on a vertical climb up the corporate ladder. He wasn't a child prodigy and didn't stay up nights dreaming of the presidency; he counted sheep instead. He was just a blue-collar shepherd. But he was a shepherd with integrity. That's what separated him from the hirelings and the hucksters. Undoubtedly, that's why God chose him to shepherd His people. And once he was king, David proved time and again that he was still a man of integrity.

The person with integrity has the humility of a servant and is faithful in little things. Take the scalpel and probe a little deeper. Is serving a motivation in your life? If so, do you do it with humility? Or do you toot your own horn about it? And when you serve, do you serve faithfully? When no one's looking, could you still stamp your work with the seal of integrity? Would it pass inspection even though no one's inspecting?

David was noted for his integrity of heart, not because he was always righteous or spiritually healthy, but because he continually put himself on the operating table for exploratory surgery, under the watchful care of the Surgeon General Himself.

Search me, O God, and know my heart;
Try me and know my anxious thoughts;
And see if there be any hurtful way in me,
And lead me in the everlasting way. (Ps. 139:23–24)

If we want to have the integrity David had, we, too, must continually lay our hearts bare before God. We must endure His scrutiny—and, if need be, His scalpel.

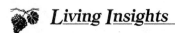

Living Insights

Prosperity tests one's integrity, an issue that is addressed in Psalms 75:4–7 and 78:70–72. To fine-tune your diagnostic skills of observation, probe each text with the following questions.

Psalm 75:4–7

Who? _____

_____

What? _____

_____

When? _____

_____

Where? _____

_____

Why? _____

_____

How? _____

_____

Psalm 78:70–72

Who? _____

_____

What? _____

_____

When? _____

_____

Where? _____

_____

Why? _____

_____

How? _____

_____

Living Insights

Perhaps the principles in this study have caused you to think of some changes that are long overdue. Let's make some plans in this direction.

- In your own words, define integrity. Afterwards, see if you can think of a person living today who demonstrated this virtue sometime during the past year. Give the specifics.

_____

_____

_____

_____

- Can you think of an example from your own life of how God has tested you with adversity? How about prosperity? Briefly describe each test and tell what you learned and how you grew.

Adversity

_____

_____

_____

_____

Prosperity

_____

_____

_____

_____

Chapter 7
STRENGTHENING YOUR GRIP ON DISCIPLESHIP

Matthew 28:16–20, Mark 3:13–14, Luke 14:25–33

The Greek word for "disciple" is *mathētēs*. It is derived from the verb *manthanō*, meaning "to learn."

> A *mathētēs* was one who attached himself to another to gain some practical or theoretical knowledge, whether by instruction or by experience. The word came to be used both of apprentices who were learning a trade and of adherents of various philosophical schools.[1]

Eugene Peterson explains the practical ramifications this word has on our relationship with Christ.

> Disciple (*mathetes*) says we are people who spend our lives apprenticed to our master, Jesus Christ. We are in a growing-learning relationship, always. A disciple is a learner, but not in the academic setting of a school-room, rather at the work site of a craftsman. We do not acquire information about God but skills in faith.[2]

To strengthen our grip on discipleship, we need hands-on experience. Book knowledge isn't enough. Classroom knowledge isn't enough. We learn from the Savior by watching Him. Seeing the compassion in His eyes as He reaches out to touch a leper. Seeing the fire in His eyes as He upends the tables of the money changers. Hearing the authority in His voice as He teaches in the synagogue. Hearing the plaintive tones in His voice as He weeps over Jerusalem.

And we learn from the Savior by walking with Him. Going where He went. Step by step, mile by mile, place by place. Walking with Him in the streets, the marketplace, the highways and byways.

---

1. Lawrence O. Richards, *Expository Dictionary of Bible Words* (Grand Rapids, Mich.: Zondervan Publishing House, 1985), p. 226.

2. Eugene H. Peterson, *A Long Obedience in the Same Direction* (Downers Grove, Ill.: InterVarsity Press, 1980), p. 13.

The Cornerstone of Discipleship

Discipleship has become something of a buzzword in Christian circles, as if it were some new management concept recently imported from the Japanese. The truth of the matter is, our commitment to discipleship stems out of a command found in Matthew 28:16–20.

> But the eleven disciples proceeded to Galilee, to the mountain which Jesus had designated. And when they saw Him, they worshiped Him; but some were doubtful. And Jesus came up and spoke to them, saying, "All authority has been given to Me in heaven and on earth. Go therefore and make disciples of all the nations, baptizing them in the name of the Father and the Son and the Holy Spirit, teaching them to observe all that I commanded you; and lo, I am with you always, even to the end of the age."

Like the last words of a retiring general to his troops, the words of Jesus have a sobering effect on His disciples—and on all today who have left their boats and nets to follow Him. "Make disciples" was His last command. This is the only imperative in these verses. All the other verbs cluster around it in a supportive way. "Go," "baptizing," and "teaching" are all dependent on the main action, to "make disciples."

The Choosing of the Disciples

Matthew 28 illustrates that the principle of discipleship is one of multiplication. First, Jesus discipled a group of apprentices; then they, in turn, were to disciple others.

But the equation first started several years earlier with the choosing of the twelve.

> And He went up to the mountain and summoned those whom He Himself wanted, and they came to Him. (Mark 3:13)

Robert Coleman tells us a little about these men's backgrounds in his outstanding book *The Master Plan of Evangelism*.

> It all started by Jesus calling a few men to follow Him. . . .
> The initial objective of Jesus' plan was to enlist men who could bear witness to His life and carry on His work after He returned to the Father. . . .

What is more revealing about these men is that at first they do not impress us as being key men. None of them occupied prominent places in the Synagogue, nor did any of them belong to the Levitical priesthood. For the most part they were common laboring men, probably having no professional training beyond the rudiments of knowledge necessary for their vocation. Perhaps a few of them came from families of some considerable means, such as the sons of Zebedee, but none of them could have been considered wealthy. They had no academic degrees in the arts and philosophies of their day. Like their Master, their formal education likely consisted only of the Synagogue schools. Most of them were raised in the poor section of the country around Galilee. Apparently the only one of the twelve who came from the more refined region of Judea was Judas Iscariot. By any standard of sophisticated culture then and now they would surely be considered as a rather ragged aggregation of souls.[3]

Sounds a lot like Paul's description of the Corinthians, doesn't it?

For consider your calling, brethren, that there were not many wise according to the flesh, not many mighty, not many noble. (1 Cor. 1:26)

Encouraging, isn't it, that Jesus chose people just like us to be His disciples—a "ragged aggregation of souls." Notice in Mark 3 *why* He chose them.

And He appointed twelve, that they might be with Him, and that He might send them out to preach. (v. 14)

The progression of verses 13 and 14 is important. There was an announcement, an appointment, and an association; *then* there was an assignment. They were involved *with* Christ before they were involved *for* Christ.

It's interesting, when you study the training techniques of Jesus, to find that He didn't require them to write anything down . . . or memorize verses . . . or rehearse methods. They were simply called to be *with* Him.

And what effect did being *with* Jesus for three-and-a-half years have on this motley group of men? Well, after a rally in Jerusalem

3. Robert E. Coleman, *The Master Plan of Evangelism* (Old Tappan, N.J.: Fleming H. Revell Co., 1964), pp. 21–23.

in which five thousand were converted, Peter and John were dragged by the religious leaders to Annas the high priest, to give an account of themselves. Filled with the Holy Spirit, Peter scathingly indicted the religious hierarchy. Instead of the religious leaders calling the disciples into account, Peter was the one who called the religious leaders on the carpet (Acts 4:4–12). Their response?

> Now as they observed the confidence of Peter and John, and understood that they were uneducated and untrained men, they were marveling, and began to recognize them as having been with Jesus. (v. 13)

That's what being with Jesus will do to a person!

The Cost of Discipleship

If being with Jesus is how we become disciples, what's the tuition for this kind of one-on-one tutoring? In Luke 14, Jesus itemizes the bill.

> Now great multitudes were going along with Him; and He turned and said to them, "If anyone comes to Me, and does not hate his own father and mother and wife and children and brothers and sisters, yes, and even his own life, he cannot be My disciple. Whoever does not carry his own cross and come after Me cannot be My disciple. For which one of you, when he wants to build a tower, does not first sit down and calculate the cost, to see if he has enough to complete it? Otherwise, when he has laid a foundation, and is not able to finish, all who observe it begin to ridicule him, saying, 'This man began to build and was not able to finish.' Or what king, when he sets out to meet another king in battle, will not first sit down and take counsel whether he is strong enough with ten thousand men to encounter the one coming against him with twenty thousand? Or else, while the other is still far away, he sends a delegation and asks terms of peace. So therefore, no one of you can be My disciple who does not give up all his own possessions. (vv. 25–33)

Jesus doesn't hand the disciples any recruiting-poster rhetoric. He doesn't promise, "Enlist and see the world." He doesn't tell them, "Follow me, and be all you can be." He doesn't smile optimistically and say, "It's a great place to start."

No, Jesus tells them up front: "It's going to cost your personal relationships" (v. 26). "It's going to cost your personal goals and desires" (v. 27). "It's going to cost your personal possessions" (v. 33).

Still want to be a disciple? Count the cost. Because—*caveat emptor*—it's going to cost you everything.[4]

 ## *Living Insights*

Luke 14:25–33 spells out the terms of discipleship. Let's use our Living Insights time today to interact with this passage.

- As we look at Luke 14:25–33, we note first that Jesus speaks words designed to thin the ranks of His followers. Why would He want to do that?

_____

_____

_____

_____

- While developing this discipleship theme, Jesus addresses three particular areas that often give us trouble. Look over verses 26–33. See if you can name these three areas.

  1. _____

  2. _____

  3. _____

- Think about each briefly. Does one give you more problems than the others? Why?

_____

_____

_____

_____

_____

_____

_____

4. See Romans 12:1, 15:1–2; Phil. 2:3–4; and Luke 22:42.

- In verses 28–32, Jesus gives a couple of illustrations to clarify discipleship. Notice that in both cases someone sits down and thinks through the involvement (vv. 28, 31). What is the implication here?

_____

_____

_____

_____

 Living Insights

Many of us have grown up with the concept of discipleship, yet we have ignored it in our own lives. This is an excellent time to reconsider this valuable subject.

- Think seriously about being a part of someone else's spiritual growth. In our age of distance and isolation, the most natural thing is to operate at arm's length from one another. Think of two or three benefits connected with small-group ministries and deeper one-on-one relationships. Spend the remainder of the time in prayer. Ask God to help you reach out more and to lead you into this type of ministry during this year.

Chapter 8

STRENGTHENING YOUR GRIP ON AGING

Psalm 90, Joshua 14:6–14

T im Stafford's excellent book *As Our Years Increase* cites an interesting survey:

> Researchers Tuckmann and Lorge asked a sample of Americans how they identified themselves. Of those *over 80*, 53 percent admitted they were old; 36 percent reported that they considered themselves middle-aged, and 11 percent, young. Nearly half, that is, thought of themselves as either young or middle-aged.[1]

Even when we're over eighty, it's hard to admit we're old. Someone has come up with the following indicators, which aren't that scientific, but they do seem to be a pretty good test to let us know when we're reaching that sunset stage of life.

You know you're old when

the flight attendant offers you coffee, tea, or Milk of Magnesia.

your back goes out more than you do.

you sit in a rocking chair and can't get it started.

everything hurts, and what doesn't hurt doesn't work.

you sink your teeth into a juicy steak, and they stay there.

Sadly, our mover-and-shaker society doesn't place a very high value on those who move and shake a little slower than the rest of us. Namely, the elderly. Centuries ago, however, that was not the case. In biblical times, the elderly were respected rather than ridiculed; and gray hair was a sign of honor rather than of humiliation (Prov. 16:31).

---

1. Tim Stafford, *As Our Years Increase* (Grand Rapids, Mich.: Zondervan Publishing House, 1989), p. 15. This is an outstanding resource on how it feels to grow old, how to prepare for growing old personally, and how to care for our loved ones as they grow old.

The man unveiled in our study today is an old man. His name is Caleb. He is eighty-five years old. But as we will see, God is far from finished with him.

Human Attitudes toward Aging

Before we take a look at Caleb, let's examine several prevalent attitudes among the aging.

Uselessness

This feeling says, "I'm over the hill" . . . "I'll just be in the way" . . . "I really don't have much to contribute anymore." People with this attitude feel that, like the old clunker in the garage, they are obsolete, belonging to another era.

Guilt

"I've blown it" . . . "If only I could do it all over again" . . . "If only I had a second chance." These thoughts are often running through the minds of elderly people experiencing guilt. They are constantly paying penance for either sins of omission or sins of commission, from which there seems no release.

Self-pity

This wounded emotion falls somewhere between blame and bitterness, crying out, "Nobody cares, so why should I?"

Fear

Fear is probably the most pervasive attitude among the elderly. The fear may be about the world outside or about their worth inside. They may say about the world, "It's changing too fast for me to keep up." Or they may say about themselves, "I'm not smart anymore" or "I'm not pretty anymore."

God's Attitude toward Aging

Now we want to take our eyes off the human perspective and look at aging from a divine perspective—both in principle and in practice.

In Principle

Psalm 90 stands in the Psalter as an august peak to give us the divine perspective. Written by a senior citizen named Moses, the psalm tells us about an ageless God, older than the mountains, older than the earth, older than time itself (vv. 1–2). But in the following verses, Moses turns his attention from the eternal to the ephemeral.

Thou dost turn man back into dust,
And dost say, "Return, O children of men."
For a thousand years in Thy sight
Are like yesterday when it passes by,
Or as a watch in the night.
Thou hast swept them away like a flood, they fall
asleep;
In the morning they are like grass which sprouts
anew.
In the morning it flourishes, and sprouts anew;
Toward evening it fades, and withers away. . . .
For all our days have declined in Thy fury;
We have finished our years like a sigh.
As for the days of our life, they contain seventy
years,
Or if due to strength, eighty years,
Yet their pride is but labor and sorrow;
For soon it is gone and we fly away. (vv. 3–6, 9–10)

If our life simply withers and grows brittle like an autumn leaf, only to fall and be interred as mulch for the cold ground, why shouldn't we feel a futility about it? Why shouldn't we feel weighted down with guilt over blossoms that never were or buds that never reached fruition or fruit that spoiled on the branch? Why shouldn't we sit in the nectared ferment of self-pity? Why shouldn't we be afraid when the first frost comes to slow our sap and loosen our grip on life's slender twig?

Why shouldn't we? Because the meaning of life does not consist of how long we live, but *how* we live; not how long the growing season, but how fragrant the flower and how sweet the fruit. That's why we should soak up each day's sunshine and each day's rain. That's why we hear a prayer in verse 12 instead of a lament.

So teach us to number our days,
That we may present to Thee a heart of wisdom.

And that's why, in verse 14, we hear a song instead of a sigh.

O satisfy us in the morning with Thy lovingkindness,
That we may sing for joy and be glad all our days.

So the principle we derive from Psalm 90 is this: Since every day is a gift from God, I will live each one enthusiastically for Him.

In Practice

Caleb is a supreme example of how this principle is worked out in everyday life. In Joshua 14 we find him, at eighty-five years of age, reflecting on his past. The context of that chapter is the aftermath of Israel's conquest of the Promised Land, when Joshua is about to parcel out the land to the individual tribes. At this juncture Caleb speaks up, casting a reflective glance to the past and one of resolve to the future.

> Then the sons of Judah drew near to Joshua in Gilgal, and Caleb the son of Jephunneh the Kenizzite said to him, "You know the word which the Lord spoke to Moses the man of God concerning you and me in Kadesh-barnea. I was forty years old when Moses the servant of the Lord sent me from Kadesh-barnea to spy out the land, and I brought word back to him as it was in my heart. Nevertheless my brethren who went up with me made the heart of the people melt with fear; but I followed the Lord my God fully. So Moses swore on that day, saying, 'Surely the land on which your foot has trodden shall be an inheritance to you and to your children forever, because you have followed the Lord my God fully.' And now behold, the Lord has let me live, just as He spoke, these forty-five years, from the time that the Lord spoke this word to Moses, when Israel walked in the wilderness; and now behold, I am eighty-five years old today. I am still as strong today as I was in the day Moses sent me; as my strength was then, so my strength is now, for war and for going out and coming in. Now then, give me this hill country about which the Lord spoke on that day, for you heard on that day that Anakim were there, with great forti- fied cities; perhaps the Lord will be with me, and I shall drive them out as the Lord has spoken." So Joshua blessed him, and gave Hebron to Caleb the son of Jephunneh for an inheritance. Therefore, Hebron be- came the inheritance of Caleb the son of Jephunneh the Kenizzite until this day, because he followed the Lord God of Israel fully. (vv. 6–14)

In his speech Caleb recounts his earlier years in verses 6–9. During that time he was chosen as one of twelve for a covert mission to cross the Jordan River and spy out the enemy territory. Ten of those spies scoped out the land with only their naked eyes. Two, however—Joshua and Caleb—saw the land through the lens of faith. And through that lens they could see past the giants and fortified cities to the cornucopian fulfillment of God's promise.

When they returned from spying out the land, at the end of forty days, they proceeded to come to Moses and Aaron and to all the congregation of the sons of Israel in the wilderness of Paran, at Kadesh; and they brought back word to them and to all the congregation and showed them the fruit of the land. Thus they told him, and said, "We went in to the land where you sent us; and it certainly does flow with milk and honey, and this is its fruit. Nevertheless, the people who live in the land are strong, and the cities are fortified and very large; and moreover, we saw the descendants of Anak there. Amalek is living in the land of the Negev and the Hittites and the Jebusites and the Amorites are living in the hill country, and the Canaanites are living by the sea and by the side of the Jordan." Then Caleb quieted the people before Moses, and said, "We should by all means go up and take possession of it, for we shall surely overcome it." But the men who had gone up with him said, "We are not able to go up against the people, for they are too strong for us." So they gave out to the sons of Israel a bad report of the land which they had spied out, saying, "The land through which we have gone, in spying it out, is a land that devours its inhabitants; and all the people whom we saw in it are men of great size. There also we saw the Nephilim (the sons of Anak are part of the Nephilim); and we became like grasshoppers in our own sight, and so we were in their sight." (Numbers 13:25–33)

Back in Joshua 14, verses 10–11 cover Caleb's middle years spent in the wilderness with a stubborn and unbelieving people. They were hard years, years of coarse sand and unrelenting heat, years of austerity rather than abundance, years of promise postponed.

Finally, in verses 12–14, when others his age would look forward to being put out to pasture, he is standing on his tiptoes, craning his neck, eyes sparkling with enthusiasm as he finds still another mountain to climb.

Our Attitude toward Aging

So far, we've taken a look at aging from both a human and a divine perspective. Now let's take a minute to examine our own attitude toward aging. If Caleb, at eighty-five, could look to the future with a robust sense of challenge, shouldn't we? We may not be as physically robust as Caleb at eighty-five, but following his lead to the top of the mountain of faith, shouldn't we still view life as a challenge instead of a threat? And on our way up that mountain, shouldn't we follow the Lord fully rather than halfheartedly?

 ### *Living Insights*

Much of our dealing with age boils down to one word . . . *attitude*. It can have an effect in any stage of life—early years, middle years, or later years. Let's examine Caleb's attitude more carefully.

- We'll center our attention on Joshua 14:6–14. As you observed in the lesson, this text divides quite nicely into three parts. Reread each passage, and make observations specifically relating to Caleb's attitudes and actions during each time period.

Early Years: Verses 6–9

_____

_____

_____

_____

_____

_____

Middle Years: Verses 10–11

_____

_____

_____

_____

_____

_____

_____

_____

_____

_____

_____

_____

_____

🍇 *Living Insights*

Your response to age is entirely up to you! You can curl up, fold up, dry up, or you can look up. Really . . . the choice is ours. No matter what our age, there are two principles in this study that we need to apply.

- View life as a challenge, not a threat.

    List some areas of life that threaten you.

    1. _____

    2. _____

    3. _____

    How can you turn those threats into challenges?

    1. _____

    _____

    _____

    _____

    2. _____

    _____

    _____

    _____

3. _____

_____

_____

_____

- Follow the Lord fully, not halfheartedly.

List some areas in your life characterized by halfhearted obedience.

1. _____

2. _____

3. _____

How can you improve in those areas?

1. _____

_____

_____

_____

2. _____

_____

_____

_____

3. _____

_____

_____

_____

Chapter 9

STRENGTHENING YOUR GRIP ON PRAYER

Philippians 4:1–9, Matthew 6:5–34

Anxiety will either drive us up the wall, or to our knees. C. S. Lewis informs us, in his book *Letters to Malcolm: Chiefly on Prayer,* that even the fingernails of hands folded in prayer can be bitten to the quick.

> All may yet be well. This is true. Meanwhile you have the waiting—waiting till the X rays are developed and till the specialist has completed his observations. And while you wait, you still have to go on living—if only one could go underground, hibernate, sleep it out. And then . . . the horrible by-products of anxiety; the incessant, circular movement of the thoughts, even the Pagan temptation to keep watch for irrational omens. And one prays; but mainly such prayers as are themselves a form of anguish.[1]

Can you relate to Lewis' honest feelings about anxiety? When you pray, do you find yourself, like Martha, distracted, worried, and bothered about so many things (Luke 10:40–41)? When you get up from your knees, do you rise with a heavier heart than before your prayers?

If you answered yes to those questions, you need a stronger grip on prayer. In this chapter we will show the cause-and-effect relationship between prayer and anxiety, and how prayer can be part of the solution rather than part of the problem.

What All of Us Want but Few of Us Have

In Philippians 4, Paul addresses a specific relational problem between two women in the church. Hidden in his advice about this breach of fellowship are those things that all of us would like in our life, but few of us have—stability . . . harmony . . . joy . . . noble thoughts . . . and consistency.

---

1. C. S. Lewis, *Letters to Malcolm: Chiefly on Prayer* (New York: Harcourt Brace Jovanovich, 1964), p. 41.

Therefore, my beloved brethren whom I long to see, my joy and crown, so *stand firm* in the Lord, my beloved. I urge Euodia and I urge Syntyche to live in *harmony* in the Lord. Indeed, true comrade, I ask you also to help these women who have shared my struggle in the cause of the gospel, together with Clement also, and the rest of my fellow workers, whose names are in the book of life. *Rejoice* in the Lord always; again I will say, rejoice! . . . Finally, brethren, whatever is true, whatever is honorable, whatever is right, whatever is pure, whatever is lovely, whatever is of good repute, if there is any excellence and if anything worthy of praise, *let your mind dwell on these things. The things you have learned and received and heard and seen in me, practice these things;* and the God of peace shall be with you. (vv. 1–4, 8–9, emphasis added)

And there is one other thing in the passage that few of us have— peace. Peace with God. Peace with ourself. With our mate. With our neighbor. Peace with our past. Our present. Our future.

What robs us of peace is anxiety. Like a thief, it raises a window to slip surreptitiously into our heart . . . tiptoeing its way through every room . . . until, at last, it distracts our thoughts and steals away our peace.

What we need is some kind of spiritual surveillance system to monitor our heart. Some sort of sentry to stand watch and deter any anxieties from a forced entry. What we need is a stronger, more lasting peace than the world has to offer. What we need is divine peace—the peace of God.

Be anxious for nothing, but in everything by prayer and supplication with thanksgiving let your requests be made known to God. And the peace of God, which surpasses all comprehension, shall guard your hearts and your minds in Christ Jesus. (vv. 6–7)

What Prayer Can Become

Prayer can easily degenerate into a rote recitation. Once-genuine praise and petition can become shop-worn, wearing down to pious, metallic platitudes that grind against God's ears. Historians trace prayer's degeneration back to several first-century changes.

First, *prayer became formalized.* The Pharisees mandated that the pious should pray at least three times a day—at nine in the morning, at noon, and at three in the afternoon. Regardless of where they were, what they were doing, or who was watching. It's no surprise that the supple nature of spontaneous prayer became just another rigid wineskin.

Second, *prayer became long.* Instead of being an effervescent overflow of the heart, prayer became an empty vessel needing to be filled. And what it became filled with was words. Lots and lots of hollow, clinking words.

Third, *prayer became repetitious.* For almost every event of the day there was a designated prayer. There was a prayer for waking and another one for retiring. There was a prayer before the meal and one after the meal. There was one for a new moon, for receiving good news, for leaving the house or leaving the city. Like the animals on Old MacDonald's farm, these prayers were everywhere. The Jews even had numerous postures for prayer, from on their knees to on their face, with eyes cast either heavenward or earthward.

Warnings about Prayer

In light of these practices, it's easy to understand why Jesus said what He did about prayer in Matthew 6. The first thing He tells the people is to *watch out for hypocrisy.*

> And when you pray, you are not to be as the hypocrites; for they love to stand and pray in the synagogues and on the street corners, in order to be seen by men. Truly I say to you, they have their reward in full. But you, when you pray, go into your inner room, and when you have shut your door, pray to your Father who is in secret, and your Father who sees in secret will repay you. (vv. 5–6)

The word *hypocrite* comes from an ancient Greek word that means "one behind a mask." It comes from the theater where actors wore masks that represented the characters they were playing. It would not be uncommon for an actor to play several roles within the performance merely by changing masks. Jesus' advice? Don't be like the hypocrites. They're just actors playing roles. They pray for approval, and in the applause of the audience, they have their reward in full (see v. 1). Prayer is not to be an act of public display but of private devotion.

The second warning Jesus gives about prayer is to *watch out for meaningless repetition.*

And when you are praying, do not use meaningless repetition, as the Gentiles do, for they suppose that they will be heard for their many words. (v. 7)

Prayer was as slippery to get a grip on for the Gentile as it was for the Jew. It was not uncommon for the Gentiles to babble incoherently, or incessantly (see 1 Kings 18:26 and Acts 19:34). This form of prayer characterized the false religions of the time, but Jesus made it plain that it was not to serve as a model for His followers.

The third warning Jesus issues is to *watch out for pride.*

For if you forgive men for their transgressions, your heavenly Father will also forgive you. But if you do not forgive men, then your Father will not forgive your transgressions. (vv. 14–15)

Pride and prayer don't mix. If you are not right with your brother on earth, how will you become right with your Father in heaven? Heavy moorings will wrap around your heart, and your prayers will never get out of dock (see 5:23–24). Don't let your pride stand in the way of your going to someone to ask forgiveness. If you do, it will also stand in the way of your prayers.

What Prayer Can Do for Anxiety

Contentment erodes under the swift or steady stream of worry. In 6:25–34, Jesus addresses the subject of anxiety in an attempt to shore up the banks of our hearts.

For this reason I say to you, do not be anxious for your life, as to what you shall eat, or what you shall drink; nor for your body, as to what you shall put on. Is not life more than food, and the body than clothing? Look at the birds of the air, that they do not sow, neither do they reap, nor gather into barns, and yet your heavenly Father feeds them. Are you not worth much more than they? And which of you by being anxious can add a single cubit to his life's span? And why are you anxious about clothing? Observe how the lilies of the field grow; they do not toil nor do they spin, yet I say to you that even Solomon in all his glory did not clothe himself like one of these. But if God so arrays the grass of the field, which is alive today and tomorrow is thrown into the furnace, will He not much more do so for you, O men of little faith? Do not be anxious then, saying, "What shall we eat?" or "What

shall we drink?" or "With what shall we clothe ourselves?" For all these things the Gentiles eagerly seek;
for your heavenly Father knows that you need all these
things. But seek first His kingdom and His righteous-
ness; and all these things shall be added to you. Therefore do not be anxious for tomorrow; for tomorrow will
care for itself. Each day has enough trouble of its own.

His words lift us onto the banks for a while as the mainstream
rushes by. From that vantage point, we see, rushing below us, anxiety
over life in general (v. 25), anxiety over the basic needs of life
(vv. 28, 31), and anxiety even over the future (v. 34).

And from the banks we can see one other thing. We can see our
heavenly Father . . . as He feeds the birds of the air . . . as He
clothes the flowers of the field . . . as He watches over us and our
every need.

Knowing that our Father is also the King—well, that in itself is
enough to calm the most worried of stomachs and the most troubled
of hearts.

 Living Insights STUDY ONE

Tucked away in Christ's Sermon on the Mount are some potent
words about prayer. They are refreshing words to read, aren't they?

• For those words to make a deeper impression, turn Matthew 6:5–15
  into a prayer list. As you read through the verses, personalize
  them as you pray, inserting your name and your own circumstances into the passage. When you come to the Lord's prayer,
  linger over each phrase and absorb it into your life. Don't race
  through it or recite it by rote. Meditate on how each request
  applies to you.

  And when you pray, you are not to be as the hypocrites;
  for they love to stand and pray in the synagogues and
  on the street corners, in order to be seen by men. Truly
  I say to you, they have their reward in full. But you,
  when you pray, go into your inner room, and when
  you have shut your door, pray to your Father who is
  in secret, and your Father who sees in secret will repay
  you. And when you are praying, do not use meaningless repetition, as the Gentiles do, for they suppose
  that they will be heard for their many words. Therefore

do not be like them; for your Father knows what you
need, before you ask Him. Pray, then, in this way:
"Our Father who art in heaven,
Hallowed be Thy name.
Thy kingdom come.
Thy will be done,
On earth as it is in heaven.
Give us this day our daily bread.
And forgive us our debts, as we also have
forgiven our debtors.
And do not lead us into temptation, but
deliver us from evil. [For Thine is the
kingdom, and the power, and the glory,
forever. Amen.]"
For if you forgive men for their transgressions, your
heavenly Father will also forgive you. But if you do
not forgive men, then your Father will not forgive your
transgressions.

Living Insights   STUDY TWO

Prayer is the answer to anxiety. Prayer is the answer to *your*
anxiety. Have you had some anxious moments recently? Have you
talked to God about them?

• In the space following, make a list of anxieties that weigh down
your life. It may include basic needs like food, shelter, or clothing. Or it may include anxiety over the future, life in general,
or specific hardships.

• Spend the remainder of the time in prayer. Under each anxiety,
write in a specific request for that need. Put a check (✔) by the
request as you pray for it. And remember to leave it in God's
hands after you've prayed.

"Be Anxious for Nothing . . ."

Anxiety _____

_____

_____ Request _____

_____

Anxiety _____

_____

_____ Request _____

_____

Anxiety _____

_____

_____ Request _____

_____

Anxiety _____

_____

_____ Request _____

_____

Anxiety _____

_____

_____ Request _____

_____

Anxiety _____

_____

_____ Request _____

_____

Chapter 10

Strengthening Your Grip on Leisure

Ephesians 5:1, Genesis 1–3

Hold it! Is your life going too fast these days?"

That's how Tim Hansel opens his classic book on leisure, *When I Relax I Feel Guilty*. He continues by asking us if we've succumbed to the workaholic, or churchaholic, rat race.

> Is it possible that your days are hurrying by so fast that you don't fully taste them anymore? Are *play* and *rest* foreign words in your living vocabulary? When was the last time you flew a kite, went for a bike ride, or made something with your hands? When was the last time you caught yourself enjoying life so deeply that you couldn't quite get the smile off your face?
> Chances are, it's been too long.[1]

How long has it been for you?

While most of us recognize the need for leisure, we have a difficult time making it a consistent part of our lives. It's especially difficult for dedicated Christian workers.

Because many Christians relentlessly drive themselves to be productive, they often view those who take a lot of leisure time as undisciplined and irresponsible. We've been programmed to believe that fatigue is next to godliness, that it's better to burn out than to rust out. But either way, we're "out." We cannot finish the race God has set before us. So we end up either on the sidelines or face down in the cinders.

Now, lest you think we're promoting a perpetual playtime, please be assured that this is not a lesson against work, but one against overwork. It's not a lesson encouraging laziness, but one encouraging leisure.

If your work has become your all-consuming interest, if it has become your greatest source of identity, worth, and security, then

1. Tim Hansel, *When I Relax I Feel Guilty* (Elgin, Ill.: David C. Cook Publishing Co., 1979), pp. 11–12.

this lesson is for you. Sit back, put your feet up, and make yourself comfortable. Allow yourself the time to get a grip on leisure.

The Place to Start: God

Most often a lack of leisure in our lives comes from a lack of balance, with the scales tipped heavily on work. To bring leisure into a more appropriate level, let's look at the Scriptures.

> Therefore be imitators of God, as beloved children. (Eph. 5:1)

The phrase *be imitators* is translated from the Greek word *mimeomai*, from which we get the word *mimic*. One scholar says the word "is always used in exhortations, and always in the continuous tense, suggesting a constant habit or practice."[2]

We are to mimic God continually and consistently, in every area. If we are to mimic God in every area, not only are we to love, forgive, and show mercy, but we're also to rest. For, as we'll explore later, even He rested upon finishing the Creation (Gen. 2:1–3).

Knowing God and imitating Him require a stillness, a slowing down, a quieting of our spirits (see Ps. 46:10, KJV). That's hard to do when work piles up, deadlines encroach, and responsibility weighs heavy on your shoulders. But look at the example of Jesus. He carried the weight of the whole world, yet He periodically took time to seek out places to be alone and away from His work (Matt. 14:23, John 6:15).

Interestingly, the word *leisure* comes from the Latin word *licere*, which means "to be permitted." We must give ourselves permission for leisure if we're ever going to make it a vital part of our lives. But many of us won't give ourselves permission until we see that leisure is a vital part of imitating God. Where in Scripture does God display His model of a balanced life? In the very first place He reveals Himself to us—the book of Genesis.

Four Guidelines from Genesis

In Genesis 1–3, God's actions give us four guidelines for cultivating leisure in our own life.

Creativity

Genesis 1:1 tells us, "In the beginning God created the heavens and the earth." From the "formless and void" (v. 2) He made beauty,

---

2. W. E. Vine, *The Expanded Vine's Expository Dictionary of New Testament Words* (Minneapolis, Minn.: Bethany House Publishers, 1984), p. 578.

order, and purpose. The oceans, the skies, the stars, the endless variety of sea and land creatures, the intricacies of the human body and brain . . . all of these were conceived in God's mind and fashioned through His fingertips.

If we are to mimic God, we must take time to create—to express that part of us that reflects our uniqueness.

When we write, when we paint, when we sculpt, when we build, when we sew, we declare most loudly our uniqueness. The act of creating lifts us above the animal kingdom to a unique role as children of God.

Communication

Later in the chapter we see that communication existed first among the members of the Godhead.

> Then God said, "Let Us make man in Our image, according to Our likeness; and let them rule over the fish of the sea and over the birds of the sky and over the cattle and over all the earth, and over every creeping thing that creeps on the earth." (v. 26)

And after creating man, God communicated with him.

> And God created man in His own image, in the image of God He created him; male and female He created them. And God blessed them; and God said to them, "Be fruitful and multiply, and fill the earth, and subdue it; and rule over the fish of the sea and over the birds of the sky, and over every living thing that moves on the earth." Then God said, "Behold, I have given you every plant yielding seed that is on the surface of all the earth, and every tree which has fruit yielding seed; it shall be food for you; and to every beast of the earth and to every bird of the sky and to every thing that moves on the earth which has life, I have given every green plant for food." (vv. 27–30)

This tells us that communication was a full expression of God's deity. God is not some blind, deaf, and mute force of nature. He is a God who sees, who hears, and who speaks. So, too, are we to communicate . . . to share, to listen, to think . . . to get to know God, ourselves, and others. This type of communication is part of a balanced life.

Rest

On the seventh day of Creation, God created the weekend!

> Thus the heavens and the earth were completed, and
> all their hosts. And by the seventh day God completed
> His work which He had done; and He rested on the
> seventh day from all His work which He had done.
> Then God blessed the seventh day and sanctified it,
> because in it He rested from all His work which God
> had created and made. (2:1–3)

He deliberately stopped working, not because He ran out of
ideas, nor because He ran out of energy. He stopped to enjoy His
creations. He made rest a priority.

How about you? Are you mimicking God in this area of your
life? Do you take time to reflect on the work of your life? We don't
mean spending the weekend on the couch, keeping up with the
Rams or the Dodgers or the Lakers. We mean time spent alone in
restful contemplation, thanking God for what you've accomplished
and for the strength and skill it took to accomplish it.

Relationships

God saw the need for Adam to have a human relationship, and
thus He created Eve (vv. 18–23). He also took the time to relate
to Adam and Eve in a personal way.

> And they heard the sound of the Lord God walking
> in the garden in the cool of the day. (3:8a)

Just as God developed a relationship by regularly meeting with
Adam and Eve in the garden, so Jesus took time to develop relationships with His disciples. He poured His life deeply into twelve
men, not broadly into twelve hundred. And within this circle of
friends, He developed a special intimacy with Peter, James, and John.

Are you cultivating friendships as part of your leisure activities?
Are you planting seeds in relationships? Are you watering others with
refreshing words of encouragement? Are you sending a little sunshine
into lives that are dark and dreary? If so, you'll see acquaintances
blossom into deeply rooted relationships that will bring years of joy.

How to Implement Leisure

Here are two suggestions to remember as you make leisure a part
of your life. First: *Deliberately stop being absorbed with the endless details
of life.* Take to heart the words of Jesus in Matthew 6, and decide

not to allow worry to rob you of God's peace (see vv. 25–34). Second: *Consciously start taking time for leisure.* Change your routine. Plan fun into your schedule. Take time to smell those proverbial roses along the way. Balance your life with creating, communicating, resting, and relating.

In closing, let these words from Orin Crane wash over your weary bones, saturating your spirit with the joy that comes from truly resting in the Lord.

Slow me down, Lord.

Ease the pounding of my heart by the quieting of my mind.

Steady my hurried pace with a vision of the eternal reach of time.

Give me, amid the confusion of the day, the calmness of the everlasting hills.

Break the tensions of my nerves and muscles with the soothing music of the singing streams that live in my memory.

Teach me the art of taking minute vacations—of slowing down to look at a flower, to chat with a friend, to pat a dog, to smile at a child, to read a few lines from a good book.

Slow me down, Lord, and inspire me to send my roots deep into the soil of life's enduring values, that I may grow toward my greater destiny.

Remind me each day that the race is not always to the swift; that there is more to life than increasing its speed.

Let me look upward to the towering oak and know that it grew great and strong because it grew slowly and well.[3]

3. Orin L. Crane, "Slow Me Down, Lord," as quoted by Tim Hansel, in *When I Relax I Feel Guilty*, p. 9.

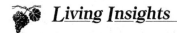

Living Insights

Ephesians 5:1–2 commands us to imitate God. Genesis 1–3 shows us the God we are to imitate. Let's use our Living Insights time today to get a better grasp on these foundational chapters.

- Read Genesis 1–3. While reading it, ask the following questions of the text. Then allow the Bible to answer for itself. Record your answers below. Remember, your primary goal in this study is to understand the character of God.

Genesis 1–3

Who? _____

_____

What? _____

_____

When? _____

_____

Where? _____

_____

Why? _____

_____

How? _____

_____

Living Insights

Maybe you've never thought of leisure as a biblical concept. Thus, maybe some more thinking in that vein is in order.

- What is there about our culture that makes us view leisure as either an enemy of the diligent or a luxury reserved for the rich? State some ways our culture refers to leisure; then briefly explain why those views are false.

False Views on Leisure

1. _____

_____

2. _____

_____

3. _____

_____

Reasons Why

_____

_____

_____

_____

_____

_____

_____

_____

_____

_____

• Leisure, stillness, silence, and rest. They all go together. They belong to one another. In light of this, read Psalm 46:10, substituting the words *have leisure* for *be still*. Then read Hebrews 4:1–11, replacing the word *rest* with *leisure*. How does this broaden your concept of leisure?

Chapter 11

STRENGTHENING YOUR GRIP ON MISSIONS
Isaiah 6:1–12

Most of us like the view from our own backyard better than from anywhere else.

Oh, we open the gate now and then to see what's happening in the world. We watch the evening news and shake our heads over public leaders' lack of integrity. We pick up the paper and spend a few minutes worrying about the rise in gang activity, or corruption among religious leaders, or the growing complacency toward pornography. We may even tune in to a talk show about the environmental effects of pollution, or have heated debates about political uprisings in faraway countries.

But a glimpse is enough—after all, we've got our own lives to lead. Maybe there's a corner of concern in the back of our minds, a little worry that wonders what the world is coming to. But mainly, we have other things to think about. We have dreams to fulfill and goals to pursue.

Isaiah probably felt the same way. Born twenty-seven centuries ago into the home of Amoz (Isa. 1:1), it's likely that he was one of Zion's aristocrats.[1] Growing up, he couldn't help but be aware of the problems in his country. He surely caught an occasional report about the mounting power of Assyria, Judah's notorious enemy. He probably sighed a little over the heathen customs spreading their roots through his society. He might have grimaced at the idolatry and immorality beginning to erode the foundations. And surely he shook his head at the sensuality of the women and the impurity of the priests.

But if Isaiah was aware of all that, he wasn't involved in it. More than likely, he had his life all mapped out, and the itinerary looked pretty good. He was off and running on his chosen path, until something got his attention.

---

1. "Because of his ready access to the court and his seeming lack of inhibition in confronting monarchs (cf. chs. 7, 36–39), scholars have often suggested that Isaiah was of noble, if not royal, descent." *The Eerdmans Bible Dictionary*, ed. Allen C. Myers (Grand Rapids, Mich.: William B. Eerdmans Publishing Co., 1987), p. 531. See also *A Survey of Old Testament Introduction*, by Gleason L. Archer, Jr. (Chicago, Ill.: Moody Press, 1964), p. 317.

And that something changed the course of his life.

Relevant Principles from an Ancient Prophet

The single event that changed Isaiah from an up-and-coming young blue blood to a downcast prophet of Israel happened in the wake of King Uzziah's death.

King Uzziah was one of the few righteous rulers to occupy the throne of Judah—his death was to that country what President Lincoln's was to the United States. But he also may have been Isaiah's close friend. His death may have shook Isaiah loose from the notion that the world is someone else's worry. Perhaps it was in such a moment of vulnerability that the Lord gave Isaiah a vision that redirected his life. As we study that vision, we can find five principles that pertain to us when it comes to world missions.

God uses circumstances to make us aware of His presence.

Isaiah was stunned with grief at the woes that had befallen Jerusalem. As he groped for the comfort of God, the Lord visited him in a vision.

In the year of King Uzziah's death, I saw the Lord
sitting on a throne, lofty and exalted, with the train
of His robe filling the temple. (Isa. 6:1)

Was God wringing His hands or pacing back and forth at the news of this terrible event? Not at all. With height comes perspective; He was sitting calmly on the throne in His place of authority, in absolute control.

We can blueprint our futures and construct our lives in any style we like; we can build a fence and lock the gate against the world and its unsettling needs. But we can't keep the winds of circumstance from whistling under our doors and rattling our windows, driving us to the arms of the One who can bring comfort.

Perhaps, like Isaiah, it will be the loss of a dear friend. Or maybe it will be the loss of a job or the news of a crippling illness; perhaps a sudden move or a child's accidental injury. Whatever it is, God will remind each of us that we cannot forget our need for Him. Our earthly situation will turn our eyes upward, and He will make His presence known.

God reveals His character to make us see our need.

Isaiah came to the temple in grief, but he found himself in worship as the greatness of God was revealed.

Seraphim stood above Him, each having six wings;
with two he covered his face, and with two he covered
his feet, and with two he flew. And one called out to
another and said,
> "Holy, Holy, Holy, is the Lord of hosts,
> The whole earth is full of His glory."

And the foundations of the thresholds trembled at the
voice of him who called out, while the temple was
filling with smoke. Then I said,
> "Woe is me, for I am ruined!
> Because I am a man of unclean lips,
> And I live among a people of unclean
> lips;
> For my eyes have seen the King, the Lord
> of hosts." (vv. 2–5)

It was as if a stained-glass scene had come to life, pulsating with
vibrant color, as praise thundered, shaking the rafters.

It would be hard to remember what you came for, once you had
witnessed a piece of heaven. It's interesting that Uzziah's death isn't
mentioned again in the passage—it's forgotten in Isaiah's sudden
acuity as he sees himself and his people in the light of God's infinite
holiness. Where a few moments before he'd been sleek and self-
satisfied, he now sees the truth of his condition: "a man of unclean
lips." And in the new awareness of his depravity, he feels doomed.

But one of the angels flies toward him, bearing hope in his hand.

> Then one of the seraphim flew to me, with a burning
> coal in his hand which he had taken from the altar
> with tongs. And *he touched my mouth with it* and said,
> "Behold, this has touched your lips; and your iniquity
> is taken away, and your sin is forgiven." (vv. 6–7,
> emphasis added)

Isaiah had just declared himself a man of unclean lips. It's just
possible that what Isaiah struggled with, what he hid behind as his
excuse for not serving God, was his inability to control his tongue.
Possibly he had difficulty controlling a habit of profanity.

What is it that you struggle with? Your temper? Financial insta-
bility? Immorality? There's not one of us who couldn't cry with
Isaiah, "Woe is me, for I am ruined!" Yet God specializes in taking
bruised, soiled, broken, guilty, and miserable vessels and making
them whole, forgiven, and useful again.

God gives us hope to make us realize we are useful.

The dialogue that follows takes Isaiah a step beyond affirmation to a sense of purpose.

> Then I heard the voice of the Lord, saying, "Whom shall I send, and who will go for Us?" Then I said, "Here am I. Send me!" (v. 8)

God's heart was on a world in need. He saw villages spread out like lonely islands, people stranded in a sea of despair. He could have sent His angels with the lifeline of His message, but He chose to use Isaiah. Yet, first, Isaiah needed to tear down his redwood fence and catch a vision for God's broader world program.

God expands our vision to make us evaluate our availability.

Don't miss that first word of verse 8: *then*. After the grief that brought Isaiah to his knees, after he had seen God in all His majesty —as all the things Isaiah himself wasn't, after the seraph had touched his lips with the cleansing coal, *then* God asked, "Whom shall I send?"

Up until now, Isaiah's view of the world had been limited. He'd thought of God as having Jewish features and speaking Hebrew. People outside his own circle were just part of the scenery, none of his concern. But with the death of his friend and his meeting with God, his blinders fell off to expand his peripheral vision.

God tells us the truth to make us focus on reality.

But this decision was far too important to be based on emotions alone. God sobered Isaiah's reeling heart with these words.

> "Go, and tell this people:
>> 'Keep on listening, but do not perceive;
>> Keep on looking, but do not understand.'
>> Render the hearts of this people insen-
>>> sitive,
>> Their ears dull,
>> And their eyes dim,
>> Lest they see with their eyes,
>> Hear with their ears,
>> Understand with their hearts,
>> And return and be healed."
> Then I said, "Lord, how long?" And He answered,
>> "Until cities are devastated and without
>>> inhabitant,
>> Houses are without people,

And the land is utterly desolate,
The Lord has removed men far away,
And the forsaken places are many in the
midst of the land." (vv. 9–12)

God never unconditionally promises success. He doesn't paint a rosy picture or make an offer too good to turn down. He's not looking for fortune hunters or ladder climbers; He's looking for obedience. He's looking for people willing to stop pursuing what they think will make them happy to do what will bring Him glory.

Maybe the benefit package doesn't look as good as one from a Fortune 500 company. There's no guaranteed salary, no promise of popularity or periodic promotion. But there's a sense of satisfaction and fulfillment that can never come with the pursuit of personal ambitions.

Strengthening your grip on missions requires a firm handle on reality. The greatest confirmation you need is not the tangible results of your labors but the inner assurance of being in the nucleus of God's will.

And What about You and Me . . . Today?

F. B. Meyer writes:

> In some unlikely quarter, in a shepherd's hut, or in an artizan's cottage, God has his prepared and appointed instrument. As yet the shaft is hidden in his quiver, in the shadow of his hand; but at the precise moment at which it will tell with the greatest effect, it will be produced and launched on the air.[2]

Could you be that arrow? What force in your life might take you from your snug quiver to place you on the Lord's taut bowstring?

Isn't it time you allowed Him to launch you into the broad, waiting world? Imagine the impact of one arrow, obedient to the bend of the bow, in the hands of the most almighty arms in the universe.

No wonder Isaiah volunteered with the eager words, "Here I am—send me, send me!"

2. F. B. Meyer, *David: Shepherd Psalmist—King* (Grand Rapids, Mich.: Zondervan Publishing House, 1953) p. 11.

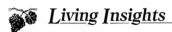

Living Insights

Isaiah 6:1–12 is Isaiah's story, but its plot is one that can be played out in each of our lives. Let's look again at the first three principles we studied. Under each one, jot down other Scripture passages that support it. Then write how each principle applies to your own life.

- God uses circumstances to make us aware of His presence.

Scriptural Support _____

_____

Appropriate Applications _____

_____

_____

_____

- God reveals His character to make us see our need.

Scriptural Support _____

_____

Appropriate Applications _____

_____

_____

_____

- God gives us hope to make us realize we are useful.

Scriptural Support _____

_____

Appropriate Applications _____

_____

_____

_____

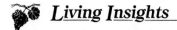

Let's continue our look at the rest of these principles regarding missions. Look for both scriptural support and some appropriate applications in your life.

• God expands our vision to make us evaluate our availability.

Scriptural Support _____

_____

Appropriate Applications _____

_____

_____

_____

• God tells us the truth to make us focus on reality.

Scriptural Support _____

_____

Appropriate Applications _____

_____

_____

_____

• Are you ready to say with Isaiah, "Here am I. Send me!"? Spend a few moments praying about this issue. What hesitations do you feel? How might they be overcome? What steps could you take to act on God's call to Isaiah—the one He places in each of our hearts? Ponder how God might use you in ways you haven't considered.

Chapter 12

Strengthening Your Grip on Godliness

1 Corinthians 10:1–13

In his poignant essay, "Life Without Principle," Henry David Thoreau writes:

> If a man walk in the woods for love of them half of each day, he is in danger of being regarded as a loafer; but if he spends his whole day as a speculator, shearing off those woods and making earth bald before her time, he is esteemed an industrious and enterprising citizen. As if a town had no interest in its forests but to cut them down![1]

Thought provoking, isn't it? And when applied to the spiritual realm, downright convicting. We have been sold a bill of goods that the committed Christian is the busy Christian—busy with people, busy with programs, busy with producing.

The problem with being so busy is that we don't often take the time to cultivate godliness, which is a private endeavor—like walking in the woods.

It is during a quiet, pensive walk through a forest that we are most likely to stand in awe of its splendor and become enraptured with its beauty. Those feelings are forged in solitude, not service. And that forging process takes time. Remember the words of the old hymn?

> Take time to be holy,
> Speak oft with thy Lord;
> Abide in Him always,
> And feed on His Word. . . .
> Take time to be holy,
> The world rushes on;
> Spend much time in secret
> With Jesus alone.[2]

1. Henry David Thoreau, "Life Without Principle," *Thoreau: Walden and Other Writings*, ed. Joseph Wood Krutch (New York, N.Y.: Bantam Books, 1962), p. 356.

2. W. D. Longstaff, "Take Time to Be Holy," *New Songs of Inspiration* (Dallas, Tex.: Zondervan Corporation, Stamps-Baxter Music, 1982), vol. 8, no. 125.

Godliness—something that's not easy to get a grip on *anyway;* but if we're busy busy busy, it's virtually impossible. With today's study we want to slow down a little, to give ourselves time to catch our breath so we can strengthen our grip on godliness.

Israel: Blessed under Moses

In 1 Corinthians 10 Paul enumerates the blessings of Israel under Moses' leadership. Miraculously delivered from the tight-knuckled grip of Pharaoh, the Israelites not only witnessed the power of God but experienced His presence and received unparalleled privileges, as well.

> For I do not want you to be unaware, brethren, that our fathers were all under the cloud, and all passed through the sea; and all were baptized into Moses in the cloud and in the sea; and all ate the same spiritual food; and all drank the same spiritual drink, for they were drinking from a spiritual rock which followed them; and the rock was Christ. (vv. 1–4)

Notice the crucial conjunction in verse 1: *for.* Contextually, this ties our passage back to the last few verses of chapter 9.

> Do you not know that those who run in a race all run, but only one receives the prize? Run in such a way that you may win. And everyone who competes in the games exercises self-control in all things. They then do it to receive a perishable wreath, but we an imperishable. Therefore I run in such a way, as not without aim; I box in such a way, as not beating the air; but I buffet my body and make it my slave, lest possibly, after I have preached to others, I myself should be disqualified. (vv. 24–27)

The imagery is instructive. Winning takes more than showing up the day of the race, slipping on a pair of Reeboks, and jogging down the track. It takes countless hours of training. It takes a special diet. And it takes an Olympic attitude of sacrificing anything that doesn't contribute to your goal.

Furthermore, it takes playing by the rules, staying in your own lane. Because if you don't, you might become disqualified. Which is exactly what happened to the Israelites.

Israel: Disqualified in the Wilderness

In spite of their excellent coach (10:2), their rigorous training (v. 1), and their spiritual diet (vv. 3–4), the Israelites wandered from the lane of obedience.

> Nevertheless, with most of them God was not well-pleased; for they were laid low in the wilderness. (v. 5)

Like runners collapsing from exhaustion during a cross-country race, the Israelites were laid low in the wilderness (see Num. 14). As a result, the vast majority of them never crossed the finish line into the Promised Land.

Israel: Swept Away by Five Narrowing Circles

The nation of Israel left behind more than bleached bones in the wilderness.

> Now these things happened as *examples* for us. (1 Cor. 10:6a, emphasis added)

The word for "example" is *tupos* in Greek. It means "to strike a blow so as to leave a mark." The word is used of nail prints in the hands of Jesus (John 20:25), and of the imprints on coins. It is used again in this passage in verse 11.

> Now these things happened to them as an example,
> and they were written for our instruction, upon whom
> the ends of the ages have come.

The word *instruction* comes from the verb meaning "to place something in the mind." Just as their lives were stamped into the Old Testament record, so the lesson of their lives should be imprinted in our thinking.

As we put their experience under the magnifying glass, we find five narrowing circles that form the swirling vortex which swept them away from God.

Circle One: Craving Evil Things

> Now these things happened as *examples* for us, that we
> should not crave evil things, as they also craved.
> (v. 6; compare Num. 11:4, 34)

This is the seductive, slow-circling outer rim of the funnel that causes us to drift from God. The closer we get to it, the more we're caught in its current—a current that sucks us inevitably and inescapably downward.

Circle Two: Idolatry

> And do not be idolaters, as some of them were; as it is written, "The people sat down to eat and drink, and stood up to play." (1 Cor. 10:7; compare Exod. 32:1–20)

Idolatry begins in the heart when we dethrone God from His position of authority in our life and enthrone some lesser god—like self, silver, or sex. The shift may be subtle, but the result is certain. It may begin with only a little homage here, a little peace offering there, but in the end it will leave us prostrate on the floor, bowing obsequiously in its presence.

Circle Three: Immorality

> Nor let us act immorally, as some of them did, and twenty-three thousand fell in one day. (1 Cor. 10:8; compare Num. 25:1–9)[3]

Immorality is "anything inconsistent with purity." It starts with our thought life and then widens to encircle others in its undertow.

Circle Four: Presuming upon God

> Nor let us try the Lord, as some of them did, and were destroyed by the serpents. (1 Cor. 10:9; compare Num. 21:4–6)

Now the circles constrict and funnel into a swifter, downward spiral, causing us to make broad, sweeping accusations against God. We become presumptuous and put God to the test.

Circle Five: Grumbling

> Nor grumble, as some of them did, and were destroyed by the destroyer. (1 Cor. 10:10; compare Num. 16:41–50)

Attitudes, good or bad, eventually express themselves verbally, for the mouth speaks from that which fills the heart (Luke 6:45). And grumbling reveals the worst of attitudes and the worst of hearts.

---

3. There is an apparent discrepancy between the accounts given by Paul and Moses. First Corinthians 10:8 gives the figure of twenty-three thousand, while Numbers 25:9 gives the figure as twenty-four thousand. Gleason L. Archer argues that Paul is not referring to the incident in Numbers 25 but rather the incident in Exodus 32:6, which the apostle quotes in verse 7. *Encyclopedia of Bible Difficulties* (Grand Rapids, Mich.: Zondervan Corporation, 1982), p. 141. This is a plausible explanation, although John W. Haley speculates that Paul *may* have intended to include only those who fell "in one day." *Alleged Discrepancies of the Bible* (1874; reprint, Nashville, Tenn.: Gospel Advocate Co., 1951), p. 382. A third option is that there was a scribal error in the copying of the text.

Notice where the progression started and where it is now. It started simply, with an attitude of craving the wrong things, which led to worshiping the wrong things, which spread to their relationships with other people, to their relationship with God—testing Him and grumbling against Him.

Common Reactions to This Instruction

As we sit back and watch the Israelites collapse in the wilderness like exhausted runners, we can take their example in either of two ways. The first is found in 1 Corinthians 10:12.

> Therefore let him who thinks he stands take heed lest he fall.

It's easy to look at the failures of others and say, "That'll never happen to me." But when we become critical about the stumblings of others, we often become cocky about our own surefootedness. And when we hoist our nose that high in the air, we set ourselves up to fall flat on our face.

The second way we might react to Israel's example is found in verse 13.

> No temptation has overtaken you but such as is common to man; and God is faithful, who will not allow you to be tempted beyond what you are able, but with the temptation will provide the way of escape also, that you may be able to endure it.

We might so identify with their sin that we feel we're in the same sinking boat with them. And we think that anything we try to change in our life is like rearranging deck chairs on the Titanic. Totally futile.

Yet that's when the Holy Spirit within us comes to the rescue, keeping too much water from inundating our life. Just as an engineer knows how much water a ship can take on before it sinks, so God knows how much temptation we can endure.

Crucial Questions for Application

A question mark has a way of imbedding its barb into our heart and not letting go. Before we close our study guide for another day, let's ask ourselves a few pointed questions.

Have you lost your delight in the Lord? Are spiritual things tasting a little dry lately? Maybe you're craving other things—the wrong things, things that aren't on the training diet.

Have you stopped taking God seriously? Can you see things you're tolerating in your life that you didn't, say, five or ten years ago? Who's on the throne of your life? Who's ruling over your passions?

Don't you know that if you keep in step with the moral meanderings of the Israelites, it will keep you in the blistering desert? Do you realize that many of them dropped in their tracks or were swallowed up by the earth or bitten by serpents or decimated by plagues?

Finally, are you willing to return to the Lord by confessing any stumbling that has caused you to fall away from Him? Are you willing to let Him touch any deadness in your spiritual life to bring about a resurrection? If you are, won't you take a few minutes to pray? That's the shortest route out of the wilderness and into the land of promise.

 Living Insights STUDY ONE

God has touched our lives in many different ways. We've been privileged to observe Him at work. Let's look in the Pentateuch at how God worked with the children of Israel.

- As you review 1 Corinthians 10:1–10, look up the accompanying Old Testament references. Jot down your observations from each.

1 Corinthians 10

Verse 1 _____

_____

_____

Exodus 13:21–22, 14:19 _____

_____

_____

Verse 2 _____

_____

_____

Exodus 14:15–22 _____

_____

_____

Verse 3 _____

_____

_____

Exodus 16:1–36 _____

_____

_____

Verse 4 _____

_____

_____

Exodus 17:1–7 _____

_____

_____

Verse 5 _____

_____

_____

Numbers 14:29, 37 _____

_____

_____

Verse 6 _____

_____

_____

Numbers 11:4 _____

_____

_____

Verse 7 _____

_____

_____

Exodus 32:1–35 _____

_____

_____

Verse 8 _____

_____

_____

Numbers 25:9 _____

_____

_____

Verse 9 _____

_____

_____

Numbers 21:4–6 _____

_____

_____

Verse 10 _____

_____

_____

Numbers 16:41–50 _____

_____

_____

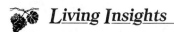

Have you thought specifically about God's blessings in your life? This includes focusing particularly upon God, the one who alone blesses.

- Spend some time writing God a letter. Let Him know exactly how you're doing. Cut through the surface stuff and get to what is _really_ happening in your life. Where there are weaknesses—and we all have them—tell God about them and how you plan to correct them. Then ask Him for strength to change.

Dear God,

_____

_____

_____

_____

_____

_____

_____

_____

_____

_____

_____

_____

_____

_____

_____

_____

Chapter 13

STRENGTHENING YOUR GRIP ON ATTITUDES

Philippians 2:1–8, 14; 4:4–8

S tripped naked, falsely accused, humiliated beneath the glare of the lights and the stare of the Gestapo, Victor Frankl stood shaved and shivering in a Nazi courtroom. His shorn head was a symbol of his shorn life: they had stolen his home, his freedom, his possessions, and had even killed his family.

Yet as Frankl faced the men who had robbed him of everything and left him with only years of indignity ahead, he realized there was one thing they could never take away.

His choice of attitude.

He could choose despair or hope, bitterness or forgiveness. He could choose to wallow in self-pity or to endure. The quality of his outer life was beaten into submission . . . but his inner life was his to rule.

Another man illustrates the importance of attitude differently— Niccolò Paganini, the gifted Italian composer and concert violinist.

One night, performing before a full house, he began to play a particularly difficult concerto. The audience sat in rapt attention. Suddenly, one of the strings on his Stradivarius snapped, and dangled uselessly beneath his bow.

Perspiration beaded his forehead. He frowned. But he continued to play, his genius lending beauty to his improvisation.

But then, unbelievably, a second string broke. And then a third. Only a single string remained taut . . . but the great musician finished the piece.

His final notes were swallowed in the wild applause of the audience. As they sank back into their seats, he waved them to silence. With a twinkle in his eye, he shouted, "Paganini . . . and one string!" And he lifted his violin and began his encore as the audience shook their heads in amazement.

Attitudes Are All-Important

The face we turn toward life is more important than any fact of life. It's more important than our past, our education, money, circumstances, appearance, talents, skills. Life is 10 percent what happens to us and 90 percent how we react to what happens.

We can't do much about the strings that dangle. But the one thing we can do is give that last string everything we've got. Paul reminds us of the importance of attitudes in his letter to the Philippians.

> If therefore there is any encouragement in Christ, if there is any consolation of love, if there is any fellowship of the Spirit, if any affection and compassion, make my joy complete by being of the same mind, maintaining the same love, united in spirit, intent on one purpose. (2:1–2)

The church at Philippi was a fairly peaceful, happy group, but apparently a few personality conflicts were starting to knock them off course. So Paul gives them some pointers to set them straight, beginning with four *ifs*. Essentially he is saying, "If you want all these things, you can have them, but you'll need to change your attitude and become of one mind. The choice is yours!"

An Attitude of Unselfish Humility

In verses 3 and 4, Paul begins to get specific.

> Do nothing from selfishness or empty conceit, but with humility of mind let each of you regard one another as more important than himself; do not merely look out for your own personal interests, but also for the interests of others.

Paul's first admonishment is to change from being self-centered to being other-centered. It's the kind of attitude Christ had when He came to earth to die for our sins.

> Have this attitude in yourselves which was also in Christ Jesus, who, although He existed in the form of God, did not regard equality with God a thing to be grasped, but emptied Himself, taking the form of a bond-servant, and being made in the likeness of men. And being found in appearance as a man, He humbled Himself by becoming obedient to the point of death, even death on a cross. (vv. 5–8)

Not an easy attitude to adopt. But did you happen to notice that little word *mind* back in verse 2? It provides the key to carrying out the command. When it comes right down to it, Jesus had to choose to come down from heaven and live among us. And it's the same with us. You can't feel humble or act humble until you think humble. Our instincts clamor, "Look out for number one," but it's only when we change our attitude that we can change our actions.

An Attitude of Positive Encouragement

In verse 14 Paul takes his advice a step further.

Do all things without grumbling or disputing.

The Greek word for *grumbling* is *goggusmos*. It even sounds like what it means, doesn't it? You can hear it every day at work—*goggusmos, goggusmos*. You can hear it in your homes, between husband and wife or brother and sister—*goggusmos, goggusmos*. You can even hear it between the church staff. If you want to *goggusmos* your way through life, you'll find plenty of company. But you'll also be discouraged, depressed, and disappointed in life. Paul exhorts us to live lives of encouragement instead by rolling up our sleeves and doing everything with a positive attitude.

An Attitude of Genuine Joy

In contrast, Paul reminds us in chapter 4 of the key to playing brilliantly when we're down to our last string.

Rejoice in the Lord always; again I will say, rejoice! Let your forbearing spirit be known to all men. (vv. 4–5a)

Rejoice? When anxiety is strapped to your shoes like lead weights?

But it doesn't say, "Rejoice in your circumstances." It says, "Rejoice in the Lord." And the next words show us how.

Be anxious for nothing, but in everything by prayer and supplication with thanksgiving let your requests be made known to God. And the peace of God, which surpasses all comprehension, shall guard your hearts and your minds in Christ Jesus. (vv. 6–7)

When we shift our load from our own shoulders to God's, anxiety drains from our hearts like water from a sieve. And in its place comes peace.

Aggressive and Passive Alternatives

When circumstances overwhelm us, we make a choice—to focus on God or to focus on problems. When we look to the problems, we generally drift either to blame or self-pity.

Blame

An aggressive response to trouble is wanting to blame someone, pinning the problem either on self, on others, or on God. But if we blame ourselves, we bind ourselves to the past, undermining our self-esteem. If we blame someone else, we alienate ourselves, poisoning our relationship with that person. If we blame God, we shut off our single most important source of help. One psychologist puts it in black-and-white terms.

> Only one kind of counselee [is] relatively hopeless: that person who blames other people for his or her problems. If you can own the mess you're in, . . . there is hope for you and help available. As long as you blame others, you will be a victim for the rest of your life.[1]

Self-pity

The passive response to trouble is self-pity. It sings that mournful little song we learned in childhood, "Nobody loves me, everybody hates me—I think I'll eat some worms." When self-pity digs in its heels, we feel victimized and hurt, too beaten to get up, as though life itself has turned on us. Our countenance hangs, as if gravity must have doubled its force.

But be careful. If you stick that lip out any further, somebody's liable to step on it!

Are you divorced? You're surrounded by others who have been divorced too. Have you failed? Welcome to the club. Have you sinned? So have we all, and God's never been more willing to forgive.

Food for the Right Attitude

In Philippians 4:8, Paul shows us how to avoid blame and self-pity by giving us six things to dwell on in their place.

> Finally, brethren, whatever is true, whatever is honor-able, whatever is right, whatever is pure, whatever is

---

1. Carl Rogers, as quoted by Bruce Larson, in *There's a lot more to health than not being sick.* (Waco, Tex.: Word Books, 1981), pp. 46–47.

lovely, whatever is of good repute, if there is any excellence and if anything worthy of praise, let your mind
dwell on these things.

Some people might call this a denial of reality. But look what
comes first on the list: whatever is *true*. The word means "reliable,
valid, honest, not deceptive or illusory." Christ doesn't want us to
live in a dream world, but in the real world, where He is in control.

Second is the word *honorable*. This is no pat-on-the-head, positive-
thinking spiel. The word means "worthy of reverence; not flippant,
cheap, superficial, or shallow."

Third is whatever is *right*—"upright and just and fair." Fourth is
whatever is *pure*—"chaste, undefiled; not smutty, shabby, or soiled."
Purity is not a high-necked dress or a pious smile. It's what can stand
the scrutiny of God.

The fifth word is *lovely*—"amiable, pleasing, agreeable." Barclay
says that the best translation of this word is actually *winsome*. [2] Maybe
we need to work on this one most of all. How winsome are you?
How agreeable to be around?

Last on the list is things that are *of good repute*. Having that
quality is the opposite of just letting it all hang out, of having a
that's-just-me-and-people-can-take-it-or-leave-it attitude. The word
means being "gracious, admirable, attractive."

Some Final Thoughts

Some of us are down to our last string. We feel stripped of all
that matters and broken beyond hope. But the real tragedy is that
we're focusing our full attention on the three strings that have
snapped. And the more we look at those frayed ends and limp,
broken strands, the more we're filled with resentment, bitterness,
sorrow, and self-pity. Remembering three final things can help us
change our focus.

First: *Our positive nature has enemies—fight them fiercely!* When
blame or self-pity, disillusionment or bitterness start weaseling their
way into your heart, push them out. You can start on your knees,
calling on the comfort of God and the power of the Holy Spirit.

Second: *Our negative nature has friends—run them off!* Other
people are glad to keep you feeling guilty, and Satan himself would

2. William Barclay, *The Letters to the Philippians, Colossians, and Thessalonians*, rev.
ed., The Daily Study Bible Series (Philadelphia, Pa.: Westminster Press, 1975), p. 80.

like to twist your thoughts and steal your peace. But it's up to you to keep your heart nourished with the forgiveness of God.

Third: *Our immediate circumstances have their purposes—let them happen!* As James tells us,

> When all kinds of trials and temptations crowd into your lives, my brothers, don't resent them as intruders, but welcome them as friends! Realise that they come to test your faith and to produce in you the quality of endurance. (James 1:2–3)[3]

We need to remember that our strength isn't in the number of strings we're playing on, but in the tune we're playing.

 Living Insights

As we've seen in our study, God is just as concerned with our attitudes as He is with our actions. Philippians 4:8 gave us six things to focus on that can rebuild our frame of mind and renew the way we live. Let's see what else Scripture has to say about these things.

- In the space below jot down other references that deal with each characteristic. Read several verses for each word or phrase; then write out your own definition for each one.

Things "True"

References _____

Definition _____

_____

Things "Honorable"

References _____

Definition _____

_____

Things "Right"

References _____

3. J. B. Phillips, The New Testament in Modern English, rev. ed., student ed. (New York, N.Y.: Macmillan Co., 1972).

91

Definition _____

_____

Things "Pure"

References _____

Definition _____

_____

Things "Lovely"

References _____

Definition _____

_____

Things "of Good Repute"

References _____

Definition _____

_____

Living Insights   STUDY TWO

Our circumstances aren't always under our control, but our attitudes always are—it's up to us to choose how we think.

- In what area of your life do you feel your attitude is good? Write
  down the things you are doing right.

_____

_____

_____

_____

_____

_____

_____

- In what area of your life do you think your attitude needs improvement? Basing your plan on the six things Paul suggests we focus on, write down ways you can change your outlook.

_____

_____

_____

_____

_____

_____

_____

Chapter 14

STRENGTHENING YOUR GRIP ON EVANGELISM

Acts 8:25–38

M ost of us Christians would rather do almost anything than witness.

There are a number of reasons for this feeling. One is *ignorance*—we don't really know how to go about it. Another is *indifference*. We have other things to think about, after all, and besides, there are plenty of evangelists out there doing the job better than we could. We're perfectly willing to pick up the tab if they'll do the job. Still another reason we're reluctant is *intimidation*. Nobody likes being made a fool of, or being asked questions they can't answer—especially by a stranger. And what if the response is hostile? The whole idea is just too scary.

And many of us have an unpleasant memory of a bad experience when someone grabbed us by the collar and shoved the gospel down our throat. We remember that embarrassed, intruded-upon, pressured feeling, and the last thing we want to do is make someone else feel that way.

Many of us have been in those situations—maybe on a plane, maybe at a convention—when the topic of religion came up and we had to face that inevitable dialogue with a nonbeliever. We've usually ended up feeling awkward and uncomfortable, and we've walked away wondering, What could I have done to not only win a hearing but keep a hearing? How could I have shown Christ to that person in a more understandable way? How could I have kept from sounding so pious or so out of touch with reality?

Good questions. And tucked away in Acts 8 is a series of answers. In this chapter is a story about a man named Philip, who was the Billy Graham of the first century. But don't let that description intimidate you—he was a layperson, like most of us, and the principles we can find in his life relate to every Christian.

Guidelines Worth Remembering

Before we look at Philip's life, there's one principle of witnessing that runs like a thread through all the others: *Put yourself in the other person's place.* If we can keep in mind that the person is coming from a different place than we are, it will help greatly.

Philip surely had this understanding, as we'll see in the encounter we're about to study. The historical background to the passage is a recent evangelistic crusade in Samaria. Christians have been proclaiming Christ from village to village, and their enthusiasm is contagious.

> And so, when they had solemnly testified and spoken the word of the Lord, they started back to Jerusalem, and were preaching the gospel to many villages of the Samaritans. (Acts 8:25)

Sensitivity

Their work couldn't have been going better. But suddenly, in verse 26, God stepped in with an unexpected directive.

> An angel of the Lord spoke to Philip saying, "Arise and go south to the road that descends from Jerusalem to Gaza." (This is a desert road.)

Here Philip is, with everything going well, when, out of the blue, God taps him on the shoulder and tells him to take off for the desert. There's no reason given, no explanation. There are no arrangements for who's to take his place in Samaria. There's just a command.

How easy it would have been for Philip to have been so caught up in the excitement of what was happening that he forgot to listen for God's voice. How tempting to brush that still, small voice away like a gnat buzzing near his ear. But Philip had walked with God long enough to know that He has a reason for throwing us a curve now and then. He was alert, ready, and sensitive to God's call.

Availability

Sensitivity has a Siamese twin—availability. There's not much good in hearing God's call if you're not willing to follow it when it comes.

> He arose and went; and behold, there was an Ethiopian eunuch, a court official of Candace, queen of the Ethiopians, who was in charge of all her treasure; and he had come to Jerusalem to worship. And he was returning and sitting in his chariot, and was reading the prophet Isaiah. (vv. 27–28)

Who would have thought it? Logic would tell you the best opportunities to witness for Christ were in the villages of Samaria, where people were flocking to hear the gospel. But out here in the middle of nowhere is a political leader sitting in his chariot and reading the Word of God. No one but God could have known how receptive this man was. His heart was ripe for harvest, so God sent one of His laborers to that faraway field. Things like that happen when we're caught up in the current of the Spirit's working.

Initiative

Still obedient, Philip follows the Holy Spirit's direction.

> And the Spirit said to Philip, "Go up and join this chariot." And when Philip had run up, he heard him reading Isaiah the prophet, and said, "Do you understand what you are reading?" (vv. 29–30)

Philip didn't wait for the man to lean out of his chariot and holler, "Excuse me, but do you happen to be an Old Testament scholar?" No. He took the initiative . . . but he took it with sensitivity. He didn't swagger up with his thumb in his suspender, toting his concordance under his arm. He didn't pull out his textbook on apologetics, ready for any argument. He wasn't out to impress or convince. He came graciously, with only one simple question.

Tactfulness

Philip's question got a straightforward answer.

> "Well, how could I, unless someone guides me?" And he invited Philip to come up and sit with him. (v. 31)

Philip didn't charge up to the chariot, wielding answers. Instead, he waited for an invitation to come and share what he knew about the Scriptures.

Witnessing sometimes seems like such an unnatural act that to accomplish it we find ourselves acting in an unnatural manner. People who are ordinarily courteous and polite, people who know which fork to use when, and how to carry on sociable small talk, suddenly become pushy and obnoxious. It's important for Christians to remember that it should be the message of the Cross that offends some people, not the messenger.

Paul Little writes wryly about his early witnessing experiences in a way many of us can relate to.

> About once every six months the pressure to witness used to reach explosive heights inside me. Not knowing any better, I would suddenly lunge at someone and spout all my verses with a sort of glazed stare in my

96

eye. I honestly didn't expect any response. As soon as my victim indicated lack of interest, I'd begin to edge away from him with a sigh of relief and the consoling thought, "All that will live godly in Christ Jesus shall suffer persecution" (II Timothy 3:12). Duty done, I'd draw back into my martyr's shell for another six months' hibernation. . . .

. . . I personally believe that parading along the sidewalk in a sandwich board which reads in large, scrawly letters, "I'm a Christian. Ask me." is not the Lord's method. He did not call us to become oddballs. As we represent Christ some people *will* think we are fools, and they will tell us so, but their opinion does not give us license to indulge in bizarre behavior.[1]

Precision

With tact, Philip let the man ask his questions without interruption. With precision, he gave the answers.

Now the passage of Scripture which he was reading was this:
> "He was led as a sheep to slaughter;
> And as a lamb before its shearer is silent,
> So He does not open His mouth.
> In humiliation His judgment was taken
>   away;
> Who shall relate His generation?
> For His life is removed from the earth."

And the eunuch answered Philip and said, "Please tell me, of whom does the prophet say this? Of himself, or of someone else?" And Philip opened his mouth, and beginning from this Scripture he preached Jesus to him. (vv. 32–35)

Even when questions sound stupid or heretical or even blasphemous, we should let them be asked. We should let people say what they need to say. Like Philip, we have to meet them on whatever road they're on and from there lead them to Calvary.

Philip didn't give the man any highfalutin philosophy; there's no record here of any "turn-or-burn" threats or scary charts about beasts and famines. There aren't even any irresistible promises of cloud-nine peace or answers to all of life's problems. There's just

---

1. Paul E. Little, *How to Give Away Your Faith* (Downers Grove, Ill.: InterVarsity Press, 1966), pp. 32, 34.

talk about Jesus—His perfect life and His sacrificial death. Philip didn't give the eunuch a course on Old Testament prophecy. He simply "preached Jesus."

It takes skill to avoid getting rabbit-trailed when you're witnessing. People have a remarkable ability to pull you off the subject and onto the pain of the world or the issue of evolution or the latest church scandal. But Jesus is truly the only issue that matters.

Decisiveness

Since Jesus is the only issue that matters, we should be decisive in putting first things first. Too often, we're so excited when someone indicates an interest that we sign them up for Christian activities before they can even shake hands with Christ Himself.

Like Philip, we need to remember to put first things first.

> And as they went along the road they came to some water; and the eunuch said, "Look! Water! What prevents me from being baptized?" [And Philip said, "If you believe with all your heart, you may." And he answered and said, "I believe that Jesus Christ is the Son of God."] And he ordered the chariot to stop; and they both went down into the water, Philip as well as the eunuch; and he baptized him. (vv. 36–38)

First there was a private acceptance of the message and *then* there was a public announcement of faith.

Closing Comments

Many Christians say to themselves, "I think God has called me to be a silent partner in winning the world to Christ. I believe He wants me to simply live my faith instead of talking about it all the time."

When it comes to witnessing, there are few things as important as living a godly life. But to say that that's all it takes is like saying a plane needs only one wing to fly. As Paul said,

> But how shall they ask [the Lord] to save them unless they believe in him? And how can they believe in him if they have never heard about him? And how can they hear about him unless someone tells them? (Rom. 10:14)[2]

2. The Living Bible (Wheaton, Ill.: Tyndale House Publishers, 1971).

God has placed you where He has placed no one else. No one else in the world has the same relationships as you. No one will stand in the same grocery store line at exactly the same moment as you. No one else will come across a hungering diplomat in the desert at exactly the same time as you.

God hasn't put you in those places merely to model the truth. Listen for the voice of the Spirit to whisper in your ear. Watch for the stranger on the road. And be aware of your opportunities to go where He would send you.

> The evangelistic harvest is always urgent. The destiny of men and of nations is always being decided. Every generation is strategic. We are not responsible for the past generation, and we cannot bear the full responsibility for the next one; but we do have our generation. God will hold us responsible as to how well we fulfill our responsibilities to this age and take advantage of our opportunities.[3]

 Living Insights

What do you think of when evangelism is mentioned? Many of us are reluctant to think seriously about this vital subject. But as our study of Acts 8 has shown us, it's a subject we can't afford to ignore.

- Since our reluctance to witness is often founded in a feeling of not knowing what to do, let's spend some time examining the action words in the passage we've been studying. Reread verses 25–38, jotting down several of the more important verbs you come to, along with each one's reference. Then write a brief statement of how each verb relates to evangelism.

Acts 8:25–38

Verb _____ Verse _____

Relation to Evangelism _____

_____

_____

3. Billy Graham, as quoted in *Quote Unquote*, comp. Lloyd Cory (Wheaton, Ill.: SP Publications, Victor Books, 1977), p. 102.

Verb _____ Verse _____

Relation to Evangelism _____

_____

_____

Verb _____ Verse _____

Relation to Evangelism _____

_____

_____

Verb _____ Verse _____

Relation to Evangelism _____

_____

_____

Verb _____ Verse _____

Relation to Evangelism _____

_____

_____

Verb _____ Verse _____

Relation to Evangelism _____

_____

_____

Verb _____ Verse _____

Relation to Evangelism _____

_____

_____

Verb _____ Verse _____

Relation to Evangelism _____

_____

_____

Verb _____ Verse _____

Relation to Evangelism _____

_____

_____

Verb _____ Verse _____

Relation to Evangelism _____

_____

_____

Verb _____ Verse _____

Relation to Evangelism _____

_____

_____

Verb _____ Verse _____

Relation to Evangelism _____

_____

_____

🍇 *Living Insights* STUDY TWO

We've spent quite a bit of time studying Philip's evangelistic encounter. Now let's take a more personal look at the subject by answering a few questions.

• Do you find evangelism difficult? If so, write down your reasons why.

_____

_____

_____

_____

_____

_____

- What preparations or principles might make evangelism easier for you? Jot down a few.

_____

_____

_____

_____

_____

_____

_____

- Is there someone in your life with whom you'd like to share the gospel? Write that person's name.

_____

Pray for an opportunity, and think through what you might say.

- What are some ways you might open the door to witnessing to a stranger?

_____

_____

_____

_____

_____

_____

_____

Chapter 15

STRENGTHENING YOUR GRIP ON AUTHORITY

1 Samuel 15:1–25

Ours is a talk-back, fight-back, get-even society of rebels. Every bastion of established authority has been stormed and taken. The character of the president has been assassinated. The image of the politician has been charred. The badge of the policeman has been ground into the dirt. The elderly have been trampled underfoot. And parents—well, just listen to this quote from James Dobson's book *Straight Talk to Men and Their Wives*:

> Humanistic theorists of our day have somehow concluded that what . . . kids need is freedom from adult leadership. Authority, even when it is permeated with love, is perceived as harmful to children.
>
> That incredible concept has given birth to a powerful political force operating within the Children's Rights Movement (CRM). Their objectives are outlined in a Child's Bill of Rights, originally written by Dr. Richard Farson, and paraphrased below:
> 1. Children should have the right to make *all* their own decisions. . . .
> 2. Children of any age should have the right to live where they choose. . . .
> 3. Children of any age should have the right to vote and be involved in any decisions that affect their lives. . . .
> 4. Children should have access to any information that is available to adults. . . .
> 5. Children should be permitted to engage in any sexual activity that is legal for their parents. . . .
> 6. Children of any age should be totally responsible for their own educational pursuits, being free to quit school or attend only when convenient. . . .
> 7. Children should have their physical environment constructed to fit their size, instead of asking them to adapt to the world of adults. . . .

8. Children should never be spanked under any circumstances, whether at school or at home.
9. Children should be guaranteed the same system of justice that now applies to adults. . . .
10. Children of any age should be permitted to join a labor union, seek employment, receive equal pay for equal work, sign legal contracts, manage all of their own money, and be financially independent. . . .

Can there be any doubt about the objective of these extreme "Children's Rights" advocates? They do not wish merely to *weaken* parental authority; they want to *kill* it, once and for all.[1]

Could the time ever be more urgent to strengthen our grip on authority?

The Roots of Rebellion

The bitter fruit of rebellion that has fallen from the laden branches of our society originated from a tiny seed. Cast from the hand of Satan, that seed first took root in the fallow hearts of Adam and Eve and then grew into a prickly, repugnant flower in the life of their son Cain. Remember that recalcitrant son's encounter with God after he had killed his brother?

> But afterwards the Lord asked Cain, "Where is your brother? Where is Abel?"
> "How should I know?" Cain retorted. "Am I supposed to keep track of him wherever he goes?"
> (Gen. 4:9)[2]

You can smell the defiance on his breath, can't you? And that defiance has seeped through the centuries until now its stench has settled onto every human relationship.

How Rebellion Reveals Itself

To strengthen our grip on authority, it will be helpful to unveil a sinister picture of rebellion closeted away in the Old Testament. It's a shadowy picture of an obsessed man—Saul. Outwardly, he is resplendently robed in the regal purples of his kingly office. But as

---

1. James C. Dobson, *Straight Talk to Men and Their Wives* (Waco, Tex.: Word Books, 1980), pp. 60–61.

2. The Living Bible (Wheaton, Ill.: Tyndale House Publishers, 1971).

we lift the veil on the portrait of his heart, we'll find a canvas brushed with burnt umber, charcoal gray, and midnight black, his *true* colors.

As we open the door to 1 Samuel 15, we'll see those colors stand out. But first let's take a look at the context surrounding that passage. In chapter 13, Saul is too impatient to wait for the priest Samuel to offer up a sacrifice, so he takes matters into his own hands and does the job himself (vv. 8–9). And doing the job *his* way is what ultimately costs him his reign (vv. 10–14). In chapter 14, Saul makes a rash vow that nearly costs his son's life (vv. 24–30, 36–45).

Four Characteristics of Rebellion

What you have in chapters 13 and 14 is Saul stepping boldly up to bat with all the braggart swagger of Casey of Mudville. With two strikes already against him, Saul dusts off his hands, chokes up on the bat, and awaits the next pitch.

In the interchange between Pitcher and batter (chap. 15), four characteristics of rebellion come to the surface. The first one emerges in verses 1–9.

Desire to Do Things My Way Instead of God's Way

The chapter opens not with a curve or a slider or a screwball. Instead, God lobs a simple pitch, as if to say, "Miss this one, Saul, and you're off the team."

> Then Samuel said to Saul, "The Lord sent me to anoint you as king over His people, over Israel; now therefore, listen to the words of the Lord. Thus says the Lord of hosts, 'I will punish Amalek for what he did to Israel, how he set himself against him on the way while he was coming up from Egypt. Now go and strike Amalek and utterly destroy all that he has, and do not spare him; but put to death both man and woman, child and infant, ox and sheep, camel and donkey.'" (vv. 1–3)

The command is straightforward, without any spin on it. Yet in the verses that follow, we'll see just how badly Saul strikes out.

> So Saul defeated the Amalekites, from Havilah as you go to Shur, which is east of Egypt. And he captured Agag the king of the Amalekites alive, and utterly destroyed all the people with the edge of the sword. But Saul and the people spared Agag and the best of

the sheep, the oxen, the fatlings, the lambs, and all that was good, and were not willing to destroy them utterly; but everything despised and worthless, that they utterly destroyed. (vv. 7–9)

God said, "Utterly destroy all." But Saul has another plan. He destroys all *except* Agag and some of the choicer livestock. There's the rebellion—see it? That subtle desire to do things our way instead of God's way. It's there, lurking in the shadows, crouching at the door to all our hearts.

Meanwhile, back in the batter's box . . . after Saul takes his third strike, God thumbs him out and sends him to the showers.

Then the word of the Lord came to Samuel, saying, "I regret that I have made Saul king, for he has turned back from following Me, and has not carried out My commands." And Samuel was distressed and cried out to the Lord all night. (1 Sam. 15:10–11)

Rationalization and Cover-up of Sin

The second characteristic of rebellion can be found in verses 12–13.

And Samuel rose early in the morning to meet Saul; and it was told Samuel, saying, "Saul came to Carmel, and behold, he set up a monument for himself, then turned and proceeded on down to Gilgal." And Samuel came to Saul, and Saul said to him, "Blessed are you of the Lord! I have carried out the command of the Lord."

People steeped in rebellion are masters of disregarding the truth and denying sin. If you compare verse 13 with verse 11, you'll see just how blatant Saul's denial is. God said to Samuel that Saul "has turned back . . . and has not carried out My commands." Yet Saul greets Samuel with a slightly altered report, "I have carried out the command of the Lord."

Isn't it remarkable how unequivocally God calls the strikes in our lives—strikes that we're so ready to call balls.

By any definition, Saul is a rationalizer. Webster defines *rationalize* in these words: "to attribute (one's actions) to rational and creditable motives without analysis of true and esp. unconscious motives . . . .to provide plausible but untrue reasons for conduct."[3]

---

3. *Webster's New Collegiate Dictionary,* see "rationalize."

But this will be one strike Saul won't be able to talk his way out of.

Defensiveness When Confronted with the Truth

Samuel confronts Saul with the truth.

> But Samuel said, "What then is this bleating of the sheep in my ears, and the lowing of the oxen which I hear?" (v. 14)

Like a kid with his hand caught in the cookie jar, Saul hastily makes up an excuse.

> And Saul said, "They have brought them from the Amalekites, for the people spared the best of the sheep and oxen, to sacrifice to the Lord your God; but the rest we have utterly destroyed." (v. 15)

His excuse is almost as believable as the child saying, "I was getting the cookies for you, Mom; really I was."

So instead of coming clean and confessing his crime, Saul merely wipes the crumbs from his face and becomes defensive.

Resistance to Accountability When Wrong Has Been Committed

By now Samuel has heard enough.

> Then Samuel said to Saul, "Wait, and let me tell you what the Lord said to me last night." And he said to him, "Speak!" And Samuel said, "Is it not true, though you were little in your own eyes, you were made the head of the tribes of Israel? And the Lord anointed you king over Israel, and the Lord sent you on a mission, and said, 'Go and utterly destroy the sinners, the Amalekites, and fight against them until they are exterminated.' Why then did you not obey the voice of the Lord, but rushed upon the spoil and did what was evil in the sight of the Lord?" Then Saul said to Samuel, "I did obey the voice of the Lord, and went on the mission on which the Lord sent me, and have brought back Agag the king of Amalek, and have utterly destroyed the Amalekites. But the people took some of the spoil, sheep and oxen, the choicest of the things devoted to destruction, to sacrifice to the Lord your God at Gilgal." (vv. 16–21)

Can you believe how Saul is passing the buck? And notice how he does it. He mixes in a little religion, which would certainly

107

appeal to a priest—"Better the animals be used for sacrifices to God than to be merely destroyed."

But Samuel doesn't buy Saul's line of reasoning.

> And Samuel said,
> "Has the Lord as much delight in burnt
> offering and sacrifices
> As in obeying the voice of the Lord?
> Behold, to obey is better than sacrifice,
> And to heed than the fat of rams.
> For rebellion is as the sin of divination,[4]
> And insubordination is as iniquity and
> idolatry.
> Because you have rejected the word of
> the Lord,
> He has also rejected you from being king."
> (vv. 22–23)

Epilogue to Rebellion

Finally, like an alcoholic coming to the point of admitting, "I am an alcoholic," Saul comes not only to an awareness of his sin, but also to his knees.

> Then Saul said to Samuel, "I have sinned; I have indeed transgressed the command of the Lord and your words, because I feared the people and listened to their voice. Now therefore, please pardon my sin and return with me, that I may worship the Lord." (vv. 24–25)

Sadly, the story ends in tragedy. In spite of his pleas, Saul had gone too far in shaking off the yoke of God's authority over his life. This was to go down as a day of infamy in the annals of biblical history. Judgment would sit on Saul's throne and pronounce its edict of rejection upon Saul's reign.

Applications to the Three Stages of Life

Rebellion is not a respecter of persons. It can be found in the palace as well as the poorhouse. It can also be found in any age, whether children, teens, or adults. In concluding today's study, we want to leave behind a principle for each of these age groups.

---

4. Divination is the practice of foretelling the future or discovering hidden knowledge by the interpretation of omens or with the aid of supernatural power through witchcraft.

Children

A rebellious nature is conceived in a home where parents relinquish control. Your children may be able to forgive all sorts of wrongs said or done to them, but this one could be the hardest (see Prov. 22:15).

Teens

A rebellious spirit is cultivated among peers who resist control (see 1 Cor. 15:33). And among adolescents, the most significant influence is their peers. Not their teachers. Not their pastors. Not even their parents.

Adults

A rebellious life is crushed by God when He regains control. If, in our adolescent years, defiance hardens and we don't learn to submit, the lessons God puts in our lives will shatter us (Prov. 1:24–32, 29:1). Only then can He take the humble pieces of our lives and reshape them.

Finally, remember the words of Samuel:

> Rebellion is as bad as the sin of witchcraft, and stubbornness is as bad as worshiping idols. (1 Sam. 15:23a)[5]

If that doesn't sober us into submission, nothing will.

 Living Insights   STUDY ONE

Ours is a rebellious world, but it didn't get that way overnight. As we've seen in our study, a defiant spirit isn't new with us. Let's look at some other Scriptures that deal with rebellion.

- Using Romans 1:18–32 as your guide, describe the cause-and-effect relationship between these acts of rebellion and their results.

Rebellion (vv. 21–23) _____

_____

_____

Results (v. 24) _____

_____

_____

5. The Living Bible.

Rebellion (v. 25) _____

_____

_____

Results (vv. 26–27) _____

_____

_____

Rebellion (v. 28a)_____

_____

_____

Results (vv. 28b–32)_____

_____

_____

- Verse 32 mentions those who "give hearty approval to those who
  practice" rebellious deeds. Is it possible to be a passive rebel? If
  so, how?

_____

_____

_____

_____

_____

_____

- Is there an area in your life in which you are passively rebelling?

_____

_____

_____

_____

_____

_____

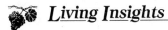

God takes a strong stand against rebellion. According to one of the Scriptures we read, rebellion is "as the sin of divination" (1 Sam. 15:23). Comparing rebellion with such a horrible sin shows God's clear feelings on the matter.

- No sin of the magnitude of rebellion "just happens." It is not a quick change. What prompts it? Are there hints that rebellion is brewing before it actually comes to the surface?

_____

_____

_____

_____

_____

_____

_____

_____

- Think about the difference between honest disagreement and overt rebellion. Can there be a genuine, necessary resistance without the presence of sinful insubordination and rebellion? Look at Acts 5:40–42 for a scriptural case in point.

_____

_____

_____

_____

_____

_____

_____

_____

- How do we resist or disagree without rebelling in the sinful sense of the word?

  _____

  _____

  _____

  _____

  _____

  _____

  _____

  _____

- What Scriptures come to mind that support your answer?

  _____

  _____

- If there is an area in your life where you struggle with rebellion, take some time to ask the Lord to help you in this dilemma.

Chapter 16

STRENGTHENING YOUR GRIP ON THE FAMILY

Psalms 127, 128

S everal years ago Edith Schaeffer wrote a book whose title asks the question, *What Is a Family?* She offered several answers, each one summarized by a chapter title. Here are a few of them:

"The Birthplace of Creativity"
"A Formation Center for Human Relationships"
"A Shelter in the Time of Storm"
"A Perpetual Relay of Truth"
"An Economic Unit"
"A Museum of Memories"
"A Door That Has Hinges and a Lock"[1]

More important than the question, What is a family? is the question, What is *your* family? What adjectives would you use to describe your home life? What holds it together?

In today's study we want to see how God describes the home. Looking at Psalms 127 and 128, we will see the unfolding of a vibrant domestic mural that chronicles the development of a healthy and happy family. That mural will serve as a pattern to help strengthen our grip on the family.

A Panoramic View

Like a fresco unfolding the four seasons before our eyes, this mural traces four distinct periods of family life. The foundation of a home is depicted in Psalm 127:1–2. The expansion of the home is sketched in verses 3–5. The years of raising children are pictured in Psalm 128:1–3. And finally, the blessings of the later years—when the children have left—are brushed in verses 4–6.

First Scene: The Foundational Years

The first two verses of Psalm 127 lay the foundation for a strong and stable home.

Unless the Lord builds the house,
They labor in vain who build it;

1. Edith Schaeffer, *What Is a Family?* (Old Tappan, N.J.: Fleming H. Revell Co., 1975).

Unless the Lord guards the city,
The watchman keeps awake in vain. (v. 1)

In Old Testament times, a city wasn't built until its walls were erected. This protected the people from any onslaught by their enemies. But the walls gave only a false sense of security. Ultimately, their fortress of trust should have been in God, not in walls (see Prov. 18:10).

The same is true for our families. Unless a husband and wife trust God with their family, their work and their watchfulness are wasted. Because, like Jericho's walls, their efforts can come tumbling down around them, and they may find themselves up to their armpits in the rubble of what was once a happy home.

Is God the builder of *your* home? Are the blueprints *His* blueprints? Are the building materials *His* materials? If not, what you're building may not really be a safe haven at all, but simply a house of cards.

Many feel that they can build a stronger home by working longer hours and providing better things for their family. But verse 2 of Psalm 127 dispels that mistaken notion.

It is vain for you to rise up early,
To retire late,
To eat the bread of painful labors;
For He gives to His beloved even in his sleep.

Burning the candle at both ends—rising early, retiring late—is futile. It is God's blessing, not our painful labors, that establishes a home. Our trust should be in His hand over our home, not in the feverish frenzy of our own hands. If our labor is to endure and prosper, we must put our hands in His.

Second Scene: The Expansion Years

A perfect illustration of God's blessings is children. And their presence marks the birth of a new stage in the home—the expansion years.

Behold, children are a gift of the Lord. (v. 3a)

The Hebrew word for *gift* means "property" or "possession." From a divine viewpoint, your children are not your own. They are God's property. He has merely appointed you as their stewards, entrusting them to your care for a brief period of time.

In the second half of verse 3, Solomon uses another image to describe children.

The fruit of the womb is a reward.

The agricultural metaphor conveys the idea that child rearing takes time, care, nurturing, and cultivation. It suggests attention rather than neglect; interest rather than irritation. Luscious fruit doesn't just happen. It's cultivated by a diligent farmer who tills, sows, waters, fertilizes, weeds, and prunes. The only things that grow well untended are weeds. Just as the harvest is the farmer's reward, so children are the parents' reward—not an interruption, another mouth to feed, a tax deduction, or a punishment.

The next picture on the mural is found in verses 4–5.

> Like arrows in the hand of a warrior,
> So are the children of one's youth.
> How blessed is the man whose quiver is full of them;
> They shall not be ashamed,
> When they speak with their enemies in the gate.

The image of arrows connotes the strength and security that children provide for their parents (see 1 Tim. 5:4). That is, if the arrows are straight and true. An arrow with a bent shaft or a blunted point offers little hope for the warrior in the heat of battle. The image of the arrow also tells us something about parenting. Skill in handling the arrow is crucial. The warrior has to know how to position the arrow on the bowstring, how much tension to place on the string, how to aim the arrow, how to adjust for the wind and distance, and finally, how to release it. The parent's skill, like that of an archer, is an exacting one. Like a warrior placing arrows in a quiver, God has placed children into your home. And if those arrows are to be launched into the world properly, then your hands must be steady, strong, and skilled.

Third Scene: The Child-Rearing Years

In the first three verses of Psalm 128, we encounter another visual description of children.

> How blessed is everyone who fears the Lord,
> Who walks in His ways.
> When you shall eat of the fruit of your hands,
> You will be happy and it will be well with you.
> Your wife shall be like a fruitful vine,
> Within your house,
> Your children like olive plants
> Around your table.

Notice how this psalm begins at the same place that Psalm 127 does—with the Lord. He is the ground from which all our blessings come. We can sow and hoe, but only He can produce the miracle of growth (see 1 Cor. 3:6–7).

And one of the blessings that issues forth from God is children. They sprout before us like "olive plants." The original Hebrew text reads, "Your children will be like *transplanted* olive shoots." At the end of nine months of gestation within the greenhouse of the womb, God takes those tender plants and transplants them into your care.

Fourth Scene: The Closing Years

The final scene on the mural of the family looks to the time of the empty nest—the time when the children have grown and gone.

> Behold, for thus shall the man be blessed
> Who fears the Lord.
> The Lord bless you from Zion,
> And may you see the prosperity of Jerusalem all the
>   days of your life.
> Indeed, may you see your *children's children.*
> Peace be upon Israel! (vv. 4–6, emphasis added)

These last verses function as a benediction that anticipates the time when the children have left home to establish homes of their own and raise their own children. Psychologists refer to this stage as the empty nest.

The empty nest can be a depressing situation for parents, but this need not be the case. If we have labored under the blessing of God and entrusted our family to Him, then the closing years of our lives should be filled with happiness and contentment—not depression.

After our children have taken flight from the nest, we will not be left with simply the nostalgia of a few downy feathers or the fragments of shells. We will be surrounded by God's blessings personally (v. 4), civically (v. 5), and nationally (v. 6).

We will still have the blessings of the Lord long after our children leave home. And we will still have our relationship with Him. After we have sent our children out into the community to be good citizens, there will be the blessing of being able to see the community benefit from such children. And finally, when this heritage is passed from us to our children to our children's children, our peace will begin to spread to the nation in which we live.

A Final Thought

"We do not judge great art. It judges us."[2] Step back from the mural of the two psalms we've studied today. Let its beauty wash over you as the images cascade into your soul. And let the images change you.

Are you building your home on the basis of a strong relationship with the Lord? Do you trust Him like you should? Do you fear Him? Are you appreciative of the gift God has given you in your children? Are you cultivating the plants God has transplanted into your care? Remember, that takes not only time but tenderness. Do you look at your children as priceless prizes God has rewarded you with? Is the love in your home unconditional? Are the memories of your home ones that both you and your children will cherish as you grow older and the nest empties?

These are pretty convicting questions. But then, the picture before us is great art. We don't judge it; it judges us. May He give us all the grace to paint a beautiful mural of *our* family. A mural so compelling it will draw not only the attention of the world but the approval of the Master Artist Himself.

 Living Insights   STUDY ONE

We've described Psalms 127 and 128 as a mural of family life. Let's look more closely at some of the details of this picture.

- Listed below are some of the words and phrases that stand out in these psalms. Scan the list and your notes, and write a brief definition of each term. If you like, go to a Bible dictionary or commentary for help. Put a check by those that are especially relevant to you.

"Builds" (127:1) _____

_____

_____

"Guards" (127:1) _____

_____

_____

---

2. Caroline Gordon, as quoted by Madeleine L'Engle, in *Walking on Water: Reflections on Faith and Art* (Wheaton, Ill.: Harold Shaw Publishers, 1980), p. 46.

"Gift" (127:3) _____

_____

_____

"Fruit" (127:3) _____

_____

_____

"Reward" (127:3) _____

_____

_____

"Arrows" (127:4) _____

_____

_____

"Fruitful vine" (128:3) _____

_____

_____

"Olive plants" (128:3) _____

_____

_____

 Living Insights

We've touched on so many valuable topics in this series of lessons on *Strengthening Your Grip*. A review is certainly in order. Let's look briefly at the sixteen areas of interest.

- Next to each topic, write down your strongest memory from the study. It may be a verse of Scripture, a practical application, a new tidbit of information, an illustration, or something of minute detail. This review will help you see where you need to be involved in strengthening your grip.

Priorities _____

_____

_____

Involvement _____

_____

_____

Encouragement _____

_____

_____

Purity _____

_____

_____

Money _____

_____

_____

Integrity _____

_____

_____

Discipleship _____

_____

_____

Aging _____

_____

_____

Prayer _____

_____

_____

Leisure _____

_____

_____

Missions _____

_____

_____

Godliness _____

_____

_____

Attitudes _____

_____

_____

Evangelism _____

_____

_____

Authority _____

_____

_____

Family _____

_____

_____

Books for Probing Further

S trengthening your grip—it's important whether you're making an approach shot with a seven-iron on the eighteenth hole, whether you're stepping up to bat, or whether you're trying to get a grasp on the big issues of life. Because sometimes the handles get a little slippery.

You may not have had a good grasp on issues such as priorities or prayer, money or missions, encouragment or evangelism. But we hope that, as a result of our study, your grip is a little more secure than it was before.

To help you continue to become more adept at handling these issues, we've included a helpful book or two for each of the sixteen topics we covered.

Priorities

MacDonald, Gordon. *Ordering Your Private World*. Nashville, Tenn.: Thomas Nelson Publishers, Oliver-Nelson, 1984.

Involvement

Stott, John. *Involvement: Being a Responsible Christian in a Non-Christian Society*. A Crucial Questions Book, vol. 1. Old Tappan, N.J.: Fleming H. Revell Co., 1985.

————. *Involvement: Social and Sexual Relationships in the Modern World*. A Crucial Questions Book, vol. 2. Old Tappan, N.J.: Fleming H. Revell, Co., 1985.

Encouragement

Crabb, Lawrence J., Jr., and Dan B. Allender. *Encouragement: The Key to Caring*. Grand Rapids, Mich.: Zondervan Publishing House, Pyranee Books, 1984.

Purity

White, Jerry. *Honesty, Morality, and Conscience*. Colorado Springs, Colo.: NavPress, 1979.

Money

Blue, Ron. *Master Your Money.* Nashville, Tenn.: Thomas Nelson Publishers, 1986.

Integrity

Wiersbe, Warren W. *The Integrity Crisis.* Nashville, Tenn.: Thomas Nelson Publishers, 1988.

Discipleship

Coleman, Robert E. *The Master Plan of Discipleship.* Old Tappan, N.J.: Fleming H. Revell Co., 1987.

Aging

Stafford, Tim. *As Our Years Increase.* Grand Rapids, Mich.: Zondervan Publishing House, Pyranee Books, 1989.

Prayer

White, John. *Daring to Draw Near.* Downers Grove, Ill.: Inter-Varsity Press, 1977.

Leisure

Hansel, Tim. *When I Relax I Feel Guilty.* Elgin, Ill.: David C. Cook Publishing Co., 1979.

Missions

Borthwick, Paul. *A Mind for Missions.* Colorado Springs, Colo.: NavPress, 1987.

Godliness

Bridges, Jerry. *The Practice of Godliness.* Colorado Springs, Colo.: NavPress, 1983.

Attitudes

Swindoll, Charles R. *Killing Giants, Pulling Thorns.* Portland, Oreg.: Multnomah Press, 1978.

Evangelism

Coleman, Robert E. *The Master Plan of Evangelism.* Old Tappan, N.J.: Fleming H. Revell Co., Power Books, 1964.

Authority

Colson, Charles W. *Loving God.* Grand Rapids, Mich.: Zondervan Publishing House, Judith Markham, 1983.

Family

Schaeffer, Edith. *What Is a Family?* Old Tappan, N.J.: Fleming H. Revell Co., 1975.

Insight for Living
Cassette Tapes
STRENGTHENING YOUR GRIP

Each decade bears a distinct characteristic. The eighties could be called the period of aimlessness. The volatile riots of the sixties and the disillusionment of the seventies produced a generation, including many Christians, that seems to have lost its way. To get back on track, we need renewed strength to dig beneath the debris of tired clichés and focus once again on certain biblical essentials. This study offers changeless, fixed points for Christians to claim—essentials in an aimless world.

			U.S.	Canada
SYG	CS	Cassette series—includes album cover ..	$44.50	$56.50
		Individual cassettes—include messages		
		A and B	5.00	6.35

These prices are subject to change without notice.

SYG	1-A:	*Strengthening Your Grip on Priorities*—1 Thessalonians 2:1–13
	B:	*Strengthening Your Grip on Involvement*—Acts 2:42–47, Romans 12:9–16, 1 Corinthians 12:20–27
SYG	2-A:	*Strengthening Your Grip on Encouragement*—Hebrews 10:19–25
	B:	*Strengthening Your Grip on Purity*—1 Thessalonians 4:1–12
SYG	3-A:	*Strengthening Your Grip on Money*—1 Timothy 6:3–19
	B:	*Strengthening Your Grip on Integrity*—Psalms 75:5–7, 78:70–72
SYG	4-A:	*Strengthening Your Grip on Discipleship*—Matthew 28:16–20, Mark 3:13–14, Luke 14:25–33
	B:	*Strengthening Your Grip on Aging*—Psalm 90, Joshua 14:6–14
SYG	5-A:	*Strengthening Your Grip on Prayer*—Philippians 4:1–9, Matthew 6:5–34
	B:	*Strengthening Your Grip on Leisure*—Ephesians 5:1, Genesis 1–3
SYG	6-A:	*Strengthening Your Grip on Missions*—Isaiah 6:1–12
	B:	*Strengthening Your Grip on Godliness*—1 Corinthians 10:1–13
SYG	7-A:	*Strengthening Your Grip on Attitudes*—Philippians 2:1–8, 14; 4:4–8
	B:	*Strengthening Your Grip on Evangelism*—Acts 8:25–38
SYG	8-A:	*Strengthening Your Grip on Authority*—1 Samuel 15:1–25
	B:	*Strengthening Your Grip on the Family*—Psalms 127, 128

How to Order by Mail

Simply mark on the order form whether you want the series or individual tapes. Mail the form with your payment to the appropriate address listed below. We will process your order as promptly as we can.

United States: Mail your order to the Sales Department at Insight for Living, Post Office Box 4444, Fullerton, California 92634. If you wish your order to be shipped first-class for faster delivery, add 10 percent of the total order amount (not including California sales tax). Otherwise, please allow four to six weeks for delivery by fourth-class mail. We accept personal checks, money orders, Visa, or MasterCard in payment for materials. Unfortunately, we are unable to offer invoicing or COD orders.

Canada: Mail your order to Insight for Living Ministries, Post Office Box 2510, Vancouver, British Columbia V6B 3W7. Please add 7 percent of your total order for first-class postage and allow approximately four weeks for delivery. Our listeners in British Columbia must also add a 6 percent sales tax to the total of all tape orders (not including postage). We accept personal checks, money orders, Visa, or MasterCard in payment for materials. Unfortunately, we are unable to offer invoicing or COD orders.

Australia, New Zealand, or Papua New Guinea: Mail your order to Insight for Living, Inc., GPO Box 2823 EE, Melbourne, Victoria 3001, Australia. Please allow six to ten weeks for delivery by surface mail. If you would like your order sent airmail, the delivery time may be reduced. Whether you choose surface or airmail, postage costs must be added to the amount of purchase and included with your order. Please use the chart that follows to determine correct postage. Due to fluctuating currency rates, we can accept only personal checks made payable in U.S. funds, international money orders, Visa, or MasterCard in payment for materials.

Overseas: Other overseas residents should contact our U.S. office. Please allow six to ten weeks for delivery by surface mail. If you would like your order sent airmail, the delivery time may be reduced. Whether you choose surface or airmail, postage costs must be added to the amount of purchase and included with your order. Please use the chart that follows to determine correct postage. Due to fluctuating currency rates, we can accept only personal checks made payable in U.S. funds, international money orders, Visa, or MasterCard in payment for materials.

Type of Postage	Postage Cost
Surface	10% of total order
Airmail	25% of total order

For Faster Service, Order by Telephone

To purchase using Visa or MasterCard, you are welcome to use our **toll-free** numbers between the hours of 8:30 A.M. and 4:00 P.M., Pacific time, Monday through Friday. The number to call from anywhere in the United States is **1-800-772-8888**. To order from Canada, call our Vancouver office at **1-800-663-7639**. Vancouver residents should call (604) 272-5811. Telephone orders from overseas are handled through our Sales Department at (714) 870-9161. We are unable to accept collect calls.

Our Guarantee

Our cassettes are guaranteed for ninety days against faulty performance or breakage due to a defect in the tape. For best results, please be sure your tape recorder is in good operating condition and is cleaned regularly.

Note: To cover processing and handling, there is a $10 fee for *any* returned check.

Order Form

SYG CS represents the entire *Strengthening Your Grip* series, while SYG 1–8 are the individual tapes included in the series.

Series or Tape	Unit Price U.S.	Canada	Quantity	Amount
SYG CS	$44.50	$56.50		$
SYG 1	5.00	6.35		
SYG 2	5.00	6.35		
SYG 3	5.00	6.35		
SYG 4	5.00	6.35		
SYG 5	5.00	6.35		
SYG 6	5.00	6.35		
SYG 7	5.00	6.35		
SYG 8	5.00	6.35		
Subtotal				
Sales tax 6% for orders delivered in California or British Columbia				
Postage 7% in Canada; overseas residents see "How to Order by Mail"				
10% optional first-class shipping and handling U.S. residents only				
Gift to Insight for Living Tax-deductible in the U.S. and Canada				
Total amount due Please do not send cash.				$

If there is a balance: ☐ apply it as a donation ☐ please refund

Form of payment:

☐ Check or money order made payable to Insight for Living
☐ Credit card (circle one): Visa   MasterCard
 Card Number _____ Expiration Date _____
 Signature _____
   We cannot process your credit card purchase without your signature.

Name _____

Address _____

City _____

State/Province _____ Zip/Postal Code _____

Country _____

Telephone ( ) _____ Radio Station ___ ___ ___ ___
   If questions arise concerning your order, we may need to contact you.

Mail this order form to the Sales Department at one of these addresses:
Insight for Living, Post Office Box 4444, Fullerton, CA 92634
Insight for Living Ministries, Post Office Box 2510, Vancouver, BC, Canada V6B 3W7
Insight for Living, Inc., GPO Box 2823 EE, Melbourne, VIC 3001, Australia

Order Form

SYG CS represents the entire *Strengthening Your Grip* series, while SYG 1–8 are the individual tapes included in the series.

Series or Tape	Unit Price U.S.	Canada	Quantity	Amount
SYG CS	$44.50	$56.50		$
SYG 1	5.00	6.35		
SYG 2	5.00	6.35		
SYG 3	5.00	6.35		
SYG 4	5.00	6.35		
SYG 5	5.00	6.35		
SYG 6	5.00	6.35		
SYG 7	5.00	6.35		
SYG 8	5.00	6.35		
Subtotal				
Sales tax 6% for orders delivered in California or British Columbia				
Postage 7% in Canada; overseas residents see "How to Order by Mail"				
10% optional first-class shipping and handling U.S. residents only				
Gift to Insight for Living Tax-deductible in the U.S. and Canada				
Total amount due Please do not send cash.				$

If there is a balance: ☐ apply it as a donation ☐ please refund

Form of payment:

☐ Check or money order made payable to Insight for Living

☐ Credit card (circle one): Visa MasterCard

Card Number _____ Expiration Date _____

Signature _____
We cannot process your credit card purchase without your signature.

Name _____

Address _____

City _____

State/Province_____ Zip/Postal Code _____

Country _____

Telephone _( )_____ Radio Station ____ ____ ____ ____
If questions arise concerning your order, we may need to contact you.

Mail this order form to the Sales Department at one of these addresses:
Insight for Living, Post Office Box 4444, Fullerton, CA 92634
Insight for Living Ministries, Post Office Box 2510, Vancouver, BC, Canada V6B 3W7
Insight for Living, Inc., GPO Box 2823 EE, Melbourne, VIC 3001, Australia